The Power of
EMOTIONAL
INTELLIGENCE

Vasant K. Agarwal

This is book is dedicated to:
My son, Dhruv, the brightest
star in the constellation
and my daughter, Sheena,
the most beautiful
lily in any father's pond.

Acknowledgement

The author is indebted to Matt Perelstein, founder
of EQ4 Peace, a philanthropic organization devoted
to education and awareness in Emotional
Intelligence worldwide. Matt has written several
Books and has videos on the subject matter, and
has given me permission to share some of his
thoughts as a contribution herein. Matt is a cancer
survivor and I wish him a speedy recovery. A
portion of the proceeds from the sale of his book
will go to his organization, as also with 'others who
are pioneering and supporting this initiative.

Your attitude, not your aptitude,
will determine your altitude.

- Zig Ziglar

In this book, the term 'EQ' and 'IQ' have been used
coincidentally to describe our overall awareness and study
of emotional intelligence, and the terms 'I', 'you', 'we' and
'us' have been used synonymously.

Table of Contents

THIS BOOK IS PRESENTED IN TWO PARTS.

Part I - **An overview of the basic concepts & fundamentals of Emotional Intelligence.**
This part is focused on teachers, student counselors, educationists and parents.

Part II - **A detailed forensic and clinical analysis of important aspects and methodology of Emotional Intelligence.**
This part is focused on all mental health professionals and counselors, trainers and   coaches.

Introduction

"Energy in Nature is a State of Physical Forces. Energy in Man is a State of Emotional Forces."

There are many definitions and interpretations of the term Emotional Intelligence and what it comprises since the main talking points and takeaways from any discussion on EI and EQ relate to the basic human quest for happiness. In our present eco-system comprising of Artificial Intelligence, Virtual Reality, Machine Learning, Augmented Reality, the key missing catalyst is Emotional Intelligence. EI is the new elephant in the room and the essence of our mental health and quest for a meaningful life.

Let us demystify this paradigm. Our educational system teaches us every subject on Earth except Happiness. Do emotions really matter? Yes, they are inherent in everything we say, do or think. Our thoughts become our feelings and:

- Effect and affect our personality, establish our self-identity, and know who we are and those around us.
- Assist in problem solving and conflict resolution.
- Enhance our communication skills so we can have 'real' conversations with others.

- Assist in consequential decision making based on the choices we make.
- Help interpret body language and non- verbal communication.
- Improve the outcome of intrapersonal and inter-personal interaction.
- Teach us how to make friends and influence people.
- Teach us empathy, compassion and humility.
- Rally your esteem, regulation, confidence & worth.
- Deliver us from our ever growing obsession with social media, cell phones and the internet.
- Help unlearn, learn and relearn.
- Maximize our human potential and life outcomes.
- Teach us how to overcome loneliness whether physical or mental.
- Understand the significance of under-thinking and over-thinking.
- Avoid over intellectualization
- Know the importance of honesty and forgiveness, without self-deception.
- Help in our careers, team building, empowerment and leadership skills.

How is our Emotional Quotient EQ related to our IQ?

Our IQ, (Intelligence Quotient) is measured by a variety of tests that measure our intellect. IQ assesses our cognitive skills such as literacy, numeracy and spatial awareness. EQ or Emotional Intelligence refers to our ability to manage our emotions and to respond effectively to other people. Like IQ, Emotional Intelligence too can be calibrated by taking a professionally designed questionnaire.

Does our Emotional Intelligence remain constant?
No, it does not. The exciting news is that we can grow and develop our Emotional Intelligence through practice and learning. It will constantly change as we grow and develop along with an understanding of our feelings and emotions. Through experience, we as humans are constantly evolving and our attitudes and emotions are changing also. Therefore, we react to a situation today differently than how we may have many years ago. The ability to identify these changes in our make-up will allow us a greater understanding of our own EI and help us to control our emotions and get the best results.

I Want to Improve my Emotional Intelligence. What should I do?
There are several solutions. For example, keeping a journal or diary to record and reflect on our

experiences. This process of reflection and recording can boost our self-awareness and self-management and propel us towards more effective responses.

We should also invite honest feedback from people we trust. This can help us to identify and act on any blind spots that may have caused us difficulty in the past. We can also work with a counselor to set goals for improving our EI. This is a very rewarding process which, with patience, will reap rewards that will transform our career and our quality of life.

The Elements of EI
1. Emotional Self Control
2. Transparency
3. Adaptability
4. Initiative
5. Optimism
6. Social Awareness
7. Empathy
8. Organizational awareness
9. Relationship management
10. Compassion
11. Providing inspirational leadership
12. Influencing
13. Being a change catalyst

14. Assisting in conflict management

15. Enhancing teamwork and collaboration

What are the Competencies of Emotional Intelligence?

Intrapersonal or invisible to others, Emotional Self-regulation, Self-awareness, Self-motivation and Interpersonal are the five competencies of our inter-personal skills which focus our attention on our own emotional state. Being aware and in the moment of what we are feeling. E.g. are we happy, excited, worried, or angry? What should (or shouldn't) we do or say next? This helps in effective decision making and to achieve better outcomes for ourselves, and others.

<u>Personal Competence</u>

Self-Awareness or knowing what we are feeling in the moment and using preferences to guide our decision making helps us understand our:

- Goals, short-term and long-term. Beliefs, self-belief and beliefs of others. Values and the things we hold dear.
- Motivators that influence and affect how we work. Abiding by the rules and regulations of society.
- Self-talk is our own knowledge that our brain tells

us when we can or cannot do something, & how they impact what we do each day.

Empathy/Social Awareness

Not to be confused with sympathy, empathy means possessing the ability to effectively put us in the other person's shoes. Not necessarily to agree but to truly understand from their point of view.

- Sensing the emotions of others. Understanding their perspective and taking an interest in their concerns
- Reading the currents, decision networks and politics at home or at work. We should choose the emotions we want to experience rather than be a victim of whatever occurs. Not letting others "push our buttons", and possess the ability to manage our emotional state. Do not confuse this with 'burying' our feelings. Rather, it is the skill to choose the emotions we want even in adversity.

Self-Management

Managing our emotions so they help us rather than hinder the task at hand is self-management. Sometimes what motivates us is hidden from our consciousness. Emotional intelligence allows us to access this information and tunes our responses or identifies our hot buttons, which when activated, evoked the 'fight' or 'flight' response reaction. This is all about being positive, and persistent rather than negative, pessimistic and doubting our decisions.

Through word and deed, we should demonstrate appreciation for others' efforts.

- Inhibiting negative action in response to anger or hostility
- Using instinct and gut feelings to be our somatic markers. These are a neurobiological under-standing of the subconscious and conscious use of 'gut feelings' which effectively guide our decisions. Could this be the essence of wisdom?

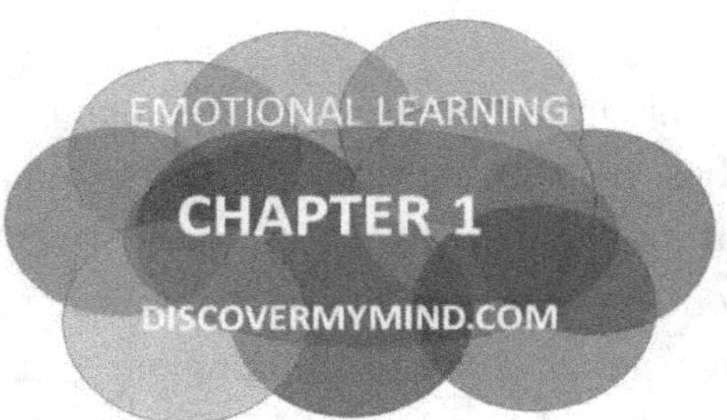

Fundamentals of Emotional Intelligence

To Explain, Explore, Ask, Involve, Measure, Behold, Know, Transcend, Appreciate, Reward, Reform, Perform, Transform, Conceive, Believe, Achieve, Identify, Understand, Recognize, Control and Regulate, all with Empathy and Compassion.

The purpose of this book is to provide education and awareness about our Emotional Quotient, or what we commonly term as EQ.

Whenever we talk about a person or describe her/him, we often comment on their intelligence. Most of us refer to 'intelligence' based on exam scores, fame or financial success. Right? We seldom describe a person in terms of their intra-personal, interpersonal or emotional intelligence? Like many, I, personally, did not pay attention to this because I came from an upbringing where my class 12 marks mattered immensely. How good I was at managing my emotions or my intelligence had little value. I am sure this is true for many of us. However, it is important to realize that there is more to intelligence than just our academic scores or fame and success.

So what is Emotional Intelligence and why is it that we know so little about it, particularly when it is one of the most important life skills we possess?

What is...Intelligence?

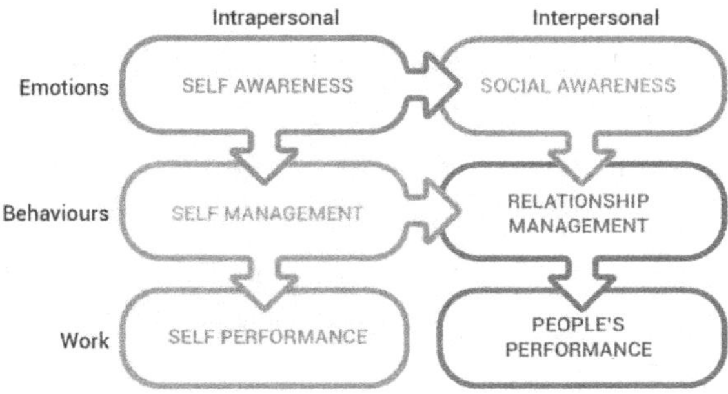

1. The power of knowing

2. The ability to understand and/or deal with new situations

3. The skilled use of reasoning

The term Emotional Intelligence was first coined by **Mayer and Salovey;** two very prominent psychologists in 1990. They defined Emotional Intelligence as **"involving the ability to monitor one's own and others' feelings and emotions, to discriminate among them and to use this information to guide one's own thinking and actions".**

According to them, emotional intelligence is

composed of four branches namely:

a. **Emotional perception**: The ability of people to attend to and perceive the variety of emotions that are expressed in a variety of situations, including body language.

b. **Emotional Integration**: This refers to the ability to access and generate feelings that facilitate thought. Our emotions are very likely to facilitate our thought process. For example when we are sad we are likely to think in a very pessimistic manner and vice versa when we are happy.

c. **Emotional Understanding**: This is the ability to understand and comprehend the implications of our emotions.

d. **Emotional Management**: This refers to the ability to regulate emotions, to be open to experiencing them and to control how they are expressed.

Thus, a person who has high emotional intelligence is likely to adapt better in her/his life since they will avoid conflict and misunderstanding. The emotionally integrated person is able to understand how emotions will affect relationships, when to avoid them or in what proportion to express them. And he or she is likely to be positive, enjoy longevity, have a flexible attitude and have high creativity.

Over the years, psychologists have developed various ways in which we can assess our emotional intelligence through a variety of psychological tests, some basic and others advanced. It is important to measure our emotional intelligence, something we have covered in detail herein.

There are various ways in which to enhance our emotional intelligence:

- **Self-monitoring**: we may keep a diary of our emotional mood change episodes; review them weekly to see what lead to negative mood changes, and how to correct the same.
- **Self-Regulation**: Self-regulations is used with self-monitoring, for avoiding depression and focusing on the non-distressing aspects. For anger, we can use the self-monitoring events that trigger anger and how to avoid them.
- **Asking someone else**: Sometimes we are unable to understand our emotions or why way we are behaving irrationally. In such situations it is important to ask someone else including friends or family for their opinion, and then work on it.

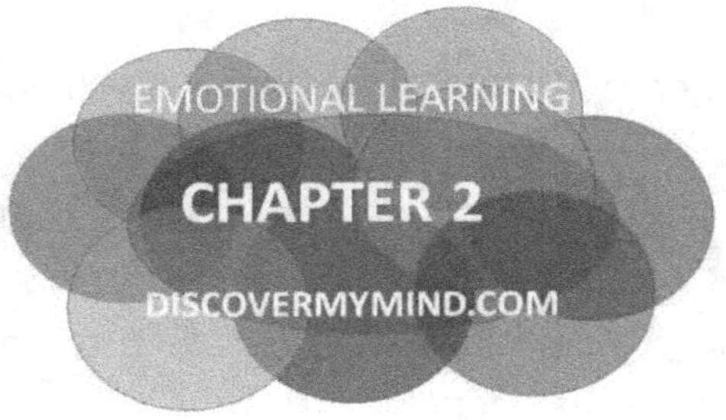

<u>Benefits of Emotional intelligence</u>

Emotions play a major and crucial role in shaping our attitude, aptitude, personality, and behavior. Thoughts, feelings and emotions get induced when we are born and evolve with time. Managing them while we are young ensures early emotional development.

It is unfortunate that parents form high expectations and focus only on grades for college placement, rather than the importance of the student's emotional health. This may result in disappointment, frustration and a low self-esteem sometimes leading to depression. Many parents are unaware that EQ is many times more important than IQ.

What is Emotional Intelligence? (EI)

Let us begin with the term emotion. Our thoughts turn into feelings which in turn evolve into emotions. They then lead to action and reaction.

All our emotions lie in our subconscious and manifest themselves based on people we meet, places we visit or events we participate in. They are known as

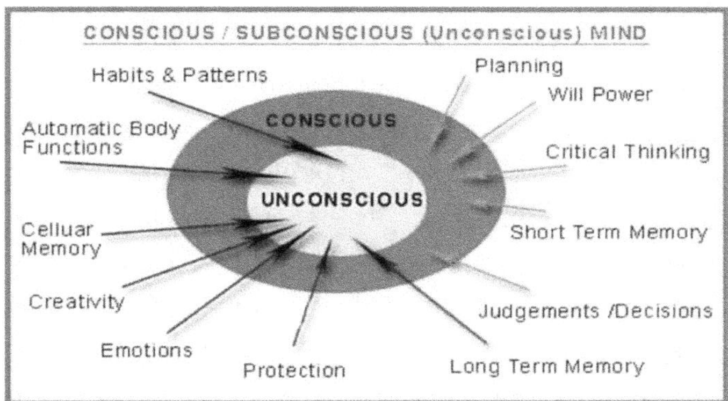

PPE. Our task is to identify, evaluate, control and express our emotions in order to achieve our maximum potential or any other preconceived objective we have in mind. Each individual has multiple intelligence, such memory logic, aptitude and personality etc., and we all have different learning abilities, some we are unaware of. It is this skillset that needs optimization as our EQ develops from our infancy to adulthood.

Why is EI important?

The subconscious or SC has no reasoning power because emotions always overpower logic, and will accept whatever it believes to be true. As opposed to the Conscious or C, it never sleeps and works 24X7. The SC is controlled by our thoughts and feelings and operates on the laws of attraction i.e. whatever is most rewarding at any given point in time. It functions based on images formed in our mind and retained by our imagination and not by words or deeds. Unlike the C, the SC cannot see or observe, be logical, rational, or make decisions. The SC has unlimited memory, rarely forgets anything and its behavior is involuntary. It works only on one thought at a time, is influenced by instant gratification, and is dominated by the five senses. When conflict occurs, the SC will overcome the C every time. While the C lives in the past and future, the SC lives only in the present.

There is a wild race in our education system today for attaining maximum scores at the expense of all other aspects of child and adolescent development. When a child does not meet parental expectations or that of their own the result is stress, mood swings, depression, and a lack of self-esteem. Often this leads to some form of addiction, be it alcohol, smoking, eating disorders, or social media. It is well known that addiction in any form is either the precursor or the aftermath of depression, derived from fear and anxiety.

If a student is not emotionally healthy, he or she will find it very difficult to be academically successful.

This is not only a fact of life but an inconvenient truth.

What are emotions?

They are the transformation of a thought into a feeling into an emotion, creating an action causing a reaction. They are the purest form of human expression.

Amongst others, there are four basic emotions: fear, anger, sadness and joy. They mirror our feelings, attitude and personality, but not our cognitive abilities. All emotions vary in degree from person to person. They impact our behavior and relationships and are the cornerstone of our social interaction.

Emotions are also significantly impacted by the environment we live in, i.e. our family, our school, who we associate with and indeed, where we reside.

People do not like emotional people. Why?

- Why is it considered more advisable to suppress emotions than to express them?
- What are the causes and consequences of emotional expression?
- Why are many people detached from their emotions?
- What turns a simple debate into argument?
- What is body language and how do we convey our emotions through non-verbal communication?

Emotions are used for both good and bad purposes and can connect, influence, convince and engage like no other medium.

So how do we manage our emotions? We can do this by recognizing and understanding the source of our emotions, by perceiving, understanding, facilitating, and managing them, and by asking how, when, and why. For example, why did someone say or not say something? Or, why did he or she do or not do something? How did I or they react to what was said, unsaid, done, or not done?

Emotions play a major and crucial role in shaping our attitude, aptitude, personality, and behavior. As mentioned, our thoughts, feelings, and emotions get induced from the time we are born, they evolve with time, and managing them during this period ensures early childhood development.

It is so unfortunate that parents form high expectations, and focus only on grades for college placement rather than the emotional health of the child. This results in disappointment, frustration, and low self-esteem, sometimes leading to depression. In fact, many parents are unaware that EQ is many times more important than IQ. If a student is emotionally unhealthy she or he can never be academically successful. This is not only a fact but an inconvenient truth.

For too long, we have focused our attention on the Intelligent Quotient, or IQ of a student as the primary benchmark for academic success. Psychologists and student counselors the world over are convinced that the emotional quotient or EQ is by far the more essential contributing component. Our multiple intelligences require that we learn and understand uniquely, and need different learning techniques if we are to assimilate and apply the knowledge gained.

If we separate the two words in Emotional Intelligence, they seem incongruous, in fact contradictory. Emotions are considered a form of self-expression without much thought, while intelligence is viewed as the core attribute of one's mental status. However, when combined, they suddenly become the basis of rational thought and action.

Understanding Emotions

Emotions contain information, and our ability to understand this information and reflect on it plays an important role in our daily life. The first task is the understanding of the complexity of emotions and the ways in which they combine (anger and disgust form contempt), progress (annoyance, anger, rage), and transition to one another.

This skill also involves the capacity to analyze emotions, their causes, and the ability to predict how people feel and react. This skill finds answers to questions such as: Why am I feeling anxious or stressed out? Why am I depressed?

Managing Emotions

The ability to regulate moods and emotions in oneself and in others constitutes the main domain of EI. When managing our feelings, we must be able to monitor, discriminate, and label our feelings accurately. Believe that we can improve or otherwise modify these feelings, employ strategies that will alter these feelings, & assess the outcome.

Since emotions are based on information, ignoring them means that we may end up making poor decisions. We need to stay open to our feelings, learn from them and use them to take appropriate action. Sometimes, it is better to disengage from emotion and return to it later. For instance anger, like many emotions is a misunderstood emotion. Anger is not necessarily a bad thing to feel. In fact, in some cases, it is anger that helps us to overcome adversity, bias, and injustice. Anger arises when we feel frustrated, cheated, or taken advantage of. Yet, if left to itself anger can blind us and cause us to act in negative or anti-social ways.

What are the causes of emotional stress?
* Parental and peer pressure.
* Relationship problems.
* Health problems
* Academic and career under performance.
* Social media addiction.

How can EI be implemented?
This should be done by educating the student, parent, school, and college on the importance and value of the approach, be it with seminars, counselor training, or in parent-teacher meetings. When we have a personal assessment in hand, the intervention can be done effectively since we are now aware of the strengths and learning abilities of the child. Parents are finding less time to devote to their child's emotional problems and simply do not know where to go or what to do. Unfortunately, schools and colleges have limited resources or willingness to take this on as a major issue.

When is a good time to start EI counseling?
Thoughts, feelings, and emotions get induced in a

person from birth and become part of our DNA. The problem is that parents with high expectations make every effort on increasing the Intelligence Quotient (IQ) of their child and sadly do not think of the Emotional Quotient (EQ). Many of them are not even aware of this, although it is now being accepted worldwide. This is the need of the hour and must be done before or during teenage years.

You may ask, what is the need of focusing on EQ in the first place? The answer is simple. If we cannot manage emotions or do not know how to control them, we face problems leading to unwanted consequences, such as:
- Improper action and reaction
- Conflict and loss of communication
- Poor academic performance
- Depression.

We should understand that our EQ is the support system for our IQ. If the EQ is high the IQ automatically benefits. Our mind stays with positive thoughts for a very short period, the rest being negative for the most part. If negative thoughts are erased through interventions, they turn into love, empathy, compassion, close relationships, and positive outcomes. The benefits of applying our EI are: Stress Management, Conflict Resolution, Social skills, Judgment Skills, Leadership Skills, Longevity,

Happiness, Self- esteem, Self-motivation, Empathy and compassion, improved performance, and much more.

Unfortunately, students are becoming emotionally challenged due to academic stress. Parents are desperately seeking solutions, leading to multiple tuitions and the purchase of learning tools for exam preparation. Many parents do not have the time or qualifications for intervention as a professionally qualified counselor can.

This is because parents have focused on the Intelligence Quotient (IQ) and not on the Emotional Quotient (EQ) as a basis for academic success. As a result, many students with any learning disability or who are underperforming in class become depressed with stress and unfounded worry. When a student is unable to realize his or her expectations or those of parents and peers, they rebel and resort to various activities as retribution. Sometimes this leads to substance abuse or an infatuation with social media. There are many incidences where EI intervention has played a key role in suicide prevention.

Each person is unique, as is the problem definition and resolution. Life is sometimes baffling, confusing, inexplicable, and unjustifiable. The answers lie partly in renewed faith and courage, increased self-confidence, and morale building. We need a total reassessment of what went wrong and why. Then the how, and why is easy. We all stumble and slip somewhere, somehow, someway or sometimes, but this must not deter us from going forward.

Life has no remote and when in trouble, we have to get up and change the channel. There are many serials to view, so switch to where there is comfort, solace, love and happiness without a 'commercial' time out! Everything has a reason. Everything! Try and find out what it is, not so much about what was right but was wrong and soon, things will start to become self-evident. This is because we either oversimplify or overcomplicate our lives.

Take a few minutes and think in depth about each of the following things we need to do:
- Renew,
- Rethink,
- Respond,
- Reflect,
- Reprogram,
- Reconnect,
- Repair,
- Restart,
- Re-evaluate,
- Reassure,
- Reach out, and
- Reconcile.

This is soul searching is most meaningful, and will hopefully provide the path to self-healing. When we go through our life experiences, four types of irrational thinking happen:

- o Euphoric Recall: The habit of remembering and exaggerating the pleasant parts of our life experiences while blocking pain or problems.
- o Magical Thinking: Imagining that life will be 'better than it was', and will result in happy days again.
- o Deriding friendly advice, noticing and exaggerating problems associated with irresponsible living, while denying and minimizing good experiences.
- o Mood and lifestyle changes: Trying to maintain a distance from other our PPE (people, places and events) while at same time wishing to relive and return to our old lifestyle right away.

"Can anyone define common sense?" The need for exercising common sense and rationality is imperative. Taking a sensible approach to identifying behavioral changes and finding out why things are the way they are. One also needs to anticipate how the other person will react and should be vigilant and proactive to prevent overreaction from either side.

In addition, finding out about our mental health by a qualified counselor is recommended. Based on their analysis, steps should be taken to pursue the most effective mode of treatment available. With significant developments in the mental health field, the diagnosis and treatment of a deferred mental condition is no more an enigma. Akin to cancer, if realize that our mental health can be managed at first indication, then the healing process will be much more effective than otherwise envisaged.

Common Sense

*A combination of our intelligence,
intuition, instinct, knowledge
and experience,
combined with our five senses.*

It is essentially our sixth sense.

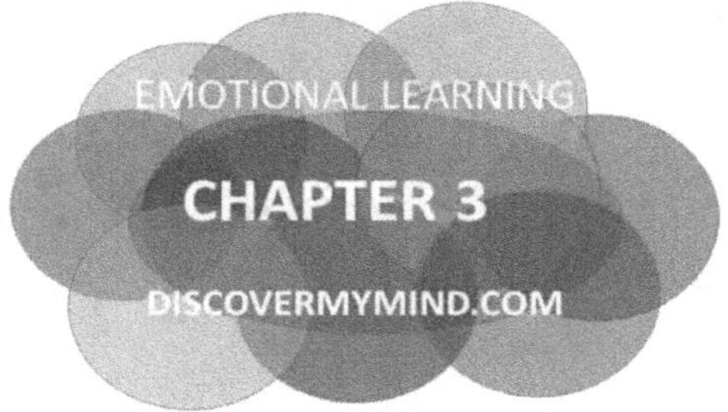

Factors affecting our Emotional Mind stream

How our thoughts impact relationship with our PPE (People, Place and   Events). Factors that impact emotional health:

- Parental expectations.
- The student's expectations.
- The internal Environment.
- The external Environment.

Behavior Management consists of:

o Identifying the person's multiple talents and skills.

o Establishing goals.

o Improving the support system with friends, family and school.

o Addressing parent or teacher issues.

o Recommending sports, extracurricular activities and social interaction.

o Avoiding peer pressure with respect to performance, i.e. grades.

o Avoiding control and manipulation.

o Enhancing communication skills.

o Empowering with motivation

o Knowing how to overcome objections.

o Mental reprograming in terms of attitude and perspective.

Behavior management involves:

- Stress Management
- Conflict Resolution
- Social skills
- Judgment skills
- Leadership skills
- Self- esteem
- Self-motivation
- Empathy and compassion

Why is Emotional Intelligence important for child development?

Thoughts, feelings and emotions get induced in us when we enter this world. They develop with time, and we must understand how to manage them at an early age, and not later. Parents, most with tall expectations of their children, make all the efforts to focus on the Intelligence Quotient (IQ) of the child, and sadly do not think of the Emotional Quotient (EQ). In fact, many of them are unaware of EI, that it has gaining ground at a swift pace worldwide, and has emerged as the need of the hour. You may ask, what is the need of focusing on EQ in the first place? The answer is clear. If we do not identify emotions and know how to control them, we will never be happy or successful

Parents should understand that EQ is the feeder factor for IQ. If EQ is higher, the IQ is automatically taken care of. It is a surprising fact that our mind stays filled with thoughts only 25% of which are positive, & the remaining being negative.

This imbalance must be reversed. When we analyze our emotions individually, we see that the sum of the parts far exceeds the whole. Let us make mind altering changes, differentiate right behavior from wrong and rid ourselves of the excess baggage of childhood trauma. Understanding emotions is the path to self-awareness and the antidote for denial. This frees us from self-imposed limits and helps achieve measurable improvement in academics, family life, careers and happiness. Mental health is possible only when we know how accept and express what we feel, which is directly related to our physical health as well.

Emotional Responsibility

We alone are responsible for our emotions and must take ownership of our thoughts, feelings, and actions. They must be managed just as we do our finances, family, relationships, success, and failure. Imagine a life without any anger or fear. Wouldn't that be wonderful?

Our Internal Operating System (IOS)

Emotions reach critical mass when they become unmanageable due to unrealistic or unfulfilled expectations. Our IOS is a part of our mental DNA, installed in our brain during our childhood and curated during adolescence. Like any other computer application, it needs to be 'debugged' and upgraded regularly. For this, we must:
   o Connect our heart to our mind.
   o Have a clear vision of who we are and what we want to be.
   o Know our goals, mission and vision in life.
   o Never allow our emotions to control our decisions.
   o Learn to forgive. It saves two souls not one.
   o Love others unconditionally.
   o Have a loving attitude and perspective in life.
   o Prioritize tasks and optimize the use of   time and resources.

Remember, happiness is an 'inside job'. Stay away from the usual suspects!

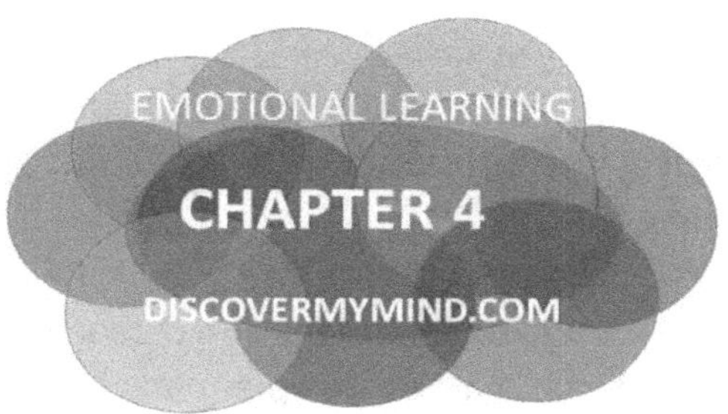

Child Development and Behavior Management

- To enrich, engage, empower, involve, motivate and inspire, with honesty, love, trust and respect. The key is communication, empathy and compassion.
- To utilize the value and application of common sense, knowledge, instinct, intuition, intelligence and experience coupled with the five senses.

This involves:

o Ego management.

o Not being in denial. Adopt, admit and accept.

o Have realistic expectations.

o Knowing the impact of people, places and events (PPE) on our behavior.

o Talking to and not at, each other. Becoming friends again.

o Knowing our present state of mind at all times i.e. our prevailing thoughts and feelings.

o Establishing our identity and character. Who are we?

o Our core beliefs and values. Self- esteem and self-

awareness.
o Thought control. What is emotional blackmail?
o Knowing the difference between a debate and an argument.
o What is our comfort zone?
o Identifying our weaknesses and correcting them.
o Knowing the games people play: a) the blame game. b) The power game.
o Avoiding fault finding and guilt tripping.
o Knowing our attitude, temperament, likes and dislikes.
o Our worries and frustrations. What is troubling us and how to deal with it?
o Our reaction to competition, both external and domestic.
o Our expectations from people, places and events.
o Fear: Who or what are we fearful of and why?
o Manipulation: How we manipulate each other.
o Sympathy, How parents and children play this trump card.
o Enabling: How this leads to excessive behavior.
o Awareness of consequences. Knowing what is right and wrong; good and bad.
o Habit formation. How, why and when it happens.
o Understanding "triggers" that affect our behavior.
o Peer pressure, and the impact of influencers. Bullying.
o Being careful of the company we keep.
o Knowing that deprivation of privileges as a form of punishment does not work.

- o Spending quality time with all those we love and care for.
- o Learning how to say 'NO'.
- o Instilling motivation and inspiration.
- o Establishing short, medium and long term goals.
- o Confidence building.
- o Removing self-doubt and worries, and elevating self-esteem.
- o Making amends. How to say thank you and sorry.
- o Showing gratitude and appreciation.

Children have what's called Multiple Intelligence, but only one or more of these learning skills is predominant, e.g. only in art, science or mathematics. When an essential area of intelligence is lacking or missing, we suffer low self-esteem and frustration. This leads to rebellion; a search of our identity and co-dependency.

Prescription medications alter the conscious which is 15% not the subconscious, which is the other 85%. The root cause of all behavior patterns lie in the subconscious. In particular, traumatic experiences related to one or more of such occurrences, become permanent subliminal fixtures that shape the personality for the rest of our life.

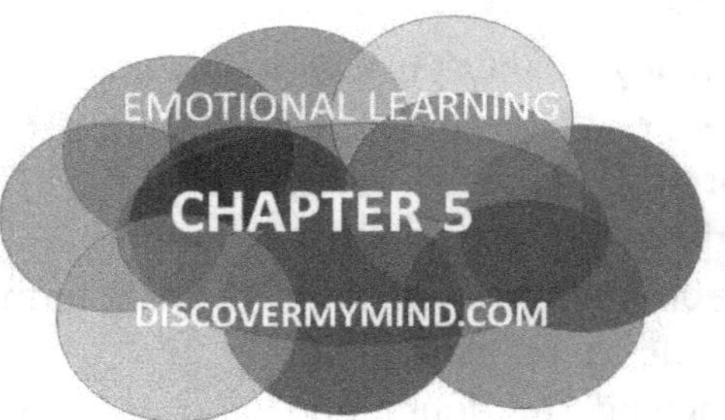

How Our Brain Works

Emotions influence our relationships, our work, our lifestyle, our sense of self, and our decisions, big and small. Here is a brief overview of the neuroscience of emotions and the different areas of the brain that are involved.

The neocortex at the front of the brain is the area we can most consciously access. It is the home of rational thought, learning, decision making, empathy and creativity. Our brain is covered by neural networks that get stronger or weaker depending on how often they are used. Those that get used repeatedly become strong 'neural pathways' which define our default thoughts, emotional profile and personality. The good news is that our neural pathways can be changed; this is called neuroplasticity.

- **Prefrontal cortex** does emotional regulation and decision-making
- **Amygdala** assesses our environment for potential

danger and conjures the anxiety, fear and anger that we might need in order to respond to potential danger, and store emotional memory so we remember painful lessons.

- **Thalamus** receives information from the senses - sight, touch, smell, hearing, taste - and sends information to relevant areas of the brain.
- **Hippocampus** is for navigation, and stores the physical sensations of emotion.

Left-brain / Right-brain

Our brain is split into two hemispheres. In general, the left-brain handles our cognitive, logical processes, while our right-brain handles our senses and emotional processes.

o The key is to become adept at using both sides of our brain to get the best information we can, and that our body is trying to give us.

o Left-brain Intellect + Right-brain Creativity = Whole-brain Living.

How our Mind Works

When we perceive something that makes us feel fear or anxiety, our thalamus sends this information to our amygdala. The amygdala checks in with our hippocampus, to see whether we have previous memories that might inform us as to how to behave in the situation now. If our hippocampus feeds back painful emotional memories, we respond with fear and anxiety.

The amygdala is needed for our survival as it can perceive danger and threat disproportionately, and flood the brain and body with the natural brain chemicals needed to fight or surrender. This is known as an 'amygdala hijack' - our emotions get so strong that we cannot think clearly - and we can find ourselves doing actions based solely on information that don't make sense logically.

Anxiety and fear lead to shallow breathing which starves the brain of oxygen, and rational thinking, creativity and empathy are abandoned. Breathing exercises can be very helpful when this happens, ensuring that our brain is receiving the oxygen it requires for functioning properly.

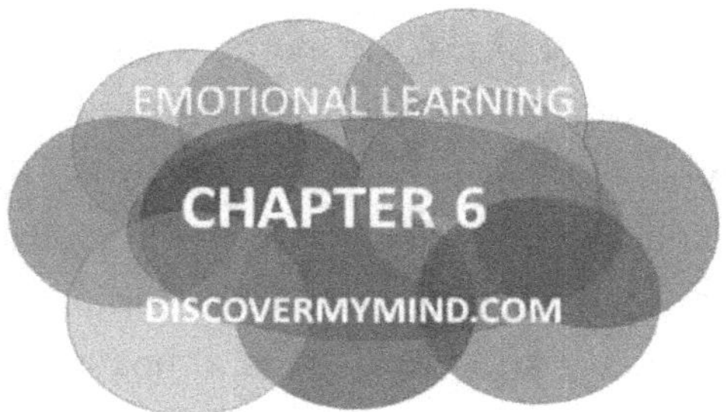

Searching for happiness - Our primary feelings are:
- Sadness
- Joy
- Anger
- Vulnerability
- Shame
- Frustration
- Helplessness
- Disappointment
- Anger
- Embarrassment
- Guilt

Components of Happiness

We are fragile in so many ways, with idiosyncrasies, penchants, and foibles as well as our inherent strengths. This is part of the human DNA. There is a plant in India called 'Chhui mui'. The moment you touch any leaf however gently, the entire plant instantly closes in on itself and becomes a tight ball, unbelievably sensitive to stimuli. It's a fern varietal called the Mimosa Pudica. We are a lot like it.

Conversely, there are the hardy cacti that can live without sustenance for months. Which of these are we and why?

Have you seen this firefly habitat in South America? Here thousands if not more of these little creations of nature light up an entire space almost brighter than the moon above. An amazing sight that made me think about the darkness of depression and how we can light up our own lives by emotional intelligence.

Happiness depends on the quality of our thoughts. Nothing is worth anything if we are not happy, and have peace of mind. They are both priceless, worth more than all the riches in the world. It is what we have, not what we want. Some people chase happiness while others choose happiness. In achieving it, we must be the doer, not the thinker, worrier, or doubter. This is done by renewing our faith, praying regularly, increasing our self-confidence, and building morale every day. T

The past cannot be allowed to steal our present or future, and we must do whatever it takes to be at peace with ourselves and our environment.

Happiness is the consequence of determining personal effort. Look for it, fight for it, strive for it, and insist upon it. Let it define, refine and outshine us.

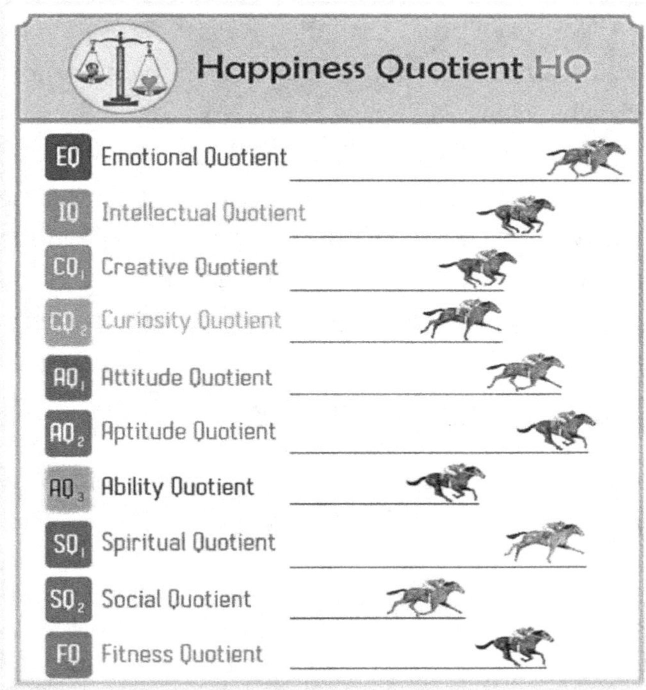

Searching for Happiness - Social interactions are one of the key drivers of happiness. Here we will find six science-backed practices to generate the most amount of happiness from your social interactions.

Respond Actively & Constructively - How we celebrate our response to someone's success is a much better predictor of strong relationships than if we ignore it.

We have four potential ways to respond when someone tells us of their success; an overview of four possible responses.

The only response that builds relationships is active-constructive. So here's what to do: Next time someone tells you about something good that happened to them, go out of your way and respond actively and constructively. Ask the person to relive the event with you — the more time he or she spends doing it, the better. And take the time to respond affirmatively.

Active-constructive	"This is great! I am so proud of you. I know how important that promotion was to you! Please relive the event with me now. Where were you when your boss told you? What did he say? How did you react? We should go out and celebrate." *Nonverbal: maintaining eye contact, displays of positive emotions such as genuine smiling, touching, laughing.*
Passive-constructive	"That is good news. You deserve it." *Nonverbal: little to no active emotional expression.*
Active-destructive	"That sounds like a lot of responsibility to take on. Are you going to spend even fewer nights at home now?" *Nonverbal: displays of negative emotions, such as furrowed brow,*

	frowning.
Passive-destructive	"So what's for dinner?" *Nonverbal: little to no eye contact, turning away, leaving the room.*

Put the Phone Away! - Research shows that the mere presence of a phone significantly diminishes the quality of your interactions even if it's muted or on airplane mode. If a phone is present, the quality of interaction is diminished. So put that phone away – in your pockets, in a bag or wherever.

Share Good News - Research shows that sharing any good news with people improves the relationship and boosts the moods of all people involved. So if you have any good news to share, go ahead and do so. Not only will you feel better, but everyone else will as well!

Give People Your Full Attention - When you're interacting with someone, make it a point to give them your full, undivided attention. Don't glance at your phone, don't look at the sky and don't be distracted by anything. At that moment, the only thing in your world is the other person. Make them feel special.

Avoid Materialism - Materialism has been shown to make people less happy, less friendly, less likable, less empathetic, less grateful, and less purposeful. Instead, it makes people more egoistic, anti-social, incompetent, and unfriendly.

The strategies below are designed to loosen materialism's grip on you, resulting in more happiness and a ton of other benefits. (Note: The practices of gratitude and mindfulness will also be beneficial in overcoming materialistic aspirations.)

Pursue Intrinsic Goals - By defining our intrinsic values (e.g., self-growth, closeness with family and friends, contribution to a greater cause) and making financial decisions based on them, we become happier and less materialistic.

Consume Useful Information - The modern world is bombarding us with materialism inducing messages all day long. One study showed that participants who were repeatedly exposed to images of luxury items, to messages that portrayed consumers rather than citizens, and to words associated with materialism (e.g. status, money, buy, asset, and expensive), experienced immediate temporary increases in anxiety, depression, and materialistic aspirations. They also became more selfish and competitive, were less inclined to join in on demanding social activities, and had an overall reduced sense of social responsibility.

To reduce our materialistic aspirations, we need to rethink our media consumption. Reduce your diet of materialism-inducing information and increase your happiness/ gratitude/ compassion/ inspiration-inducing information.

Buy the Experience, not the Goods - Spending money on experiences makes you a lot happier than spending it on "stuff."

Rather than saving for that new flat-screen TV, a faster car, better chairs, or a nicer watch, spend your money to experience life. Take up a yoga class. Hire a personal trainer. Go to Disney World with your friends or family. Take a trip to New Zealand. Visit the local theatre. Go to a concert. Invest in learning a new language. Go paintballing, bungee jumping, mountain climbing, or kite surfing.

Practice Gratitude- Practicing gratitude is a quick way to feel better about yourself and raise your level of happiness. Gratitude must be one of the best things you can ever do for yourself, as it will positively impact almost every area of your life (health, relationships, emotional life, and so on).

Write a gratitude journal. Gratitude journaling simply means writing down and reflecting on people, places, objects, memories, events you're grateful for. There's no wrong way to do this. However, there are some guidelines for getting started and tips for getting the most out of it.

Write down as many things you're grateful for as you like, ranging from the mundane (you got a lot of work done today, your husband cooked for you) to the magnificent (your book getting published or your child's first steps).

Look at things as 'gifts'- Research shows that seeing the good things in your life makes you more grateful for them. Your strengths, your health, your family, your eyes... these are all gifts given to you for free.

Got someone in mind? Now write a letter of gratitude to this individual, using the following pointers:

Address the person directly. Let the person know what you're doing now, and mention how you often remember what he or she did.

In the end, give the letter to the person for him or her to keep it. And if you don't feel like delivering the letter, don't feel bad about it. Research shows merely writing a letter is enough to create a substantial boost in happiness.

Look to the Future - Choose an experience, event, activity or even a relationship. Let's call it x. It may be ending soon.

Maybe x is a job or a class you're taking, a team you're part of or even a place where you live. With only a little time left to spend doing this or being with x, it's a chapter of your life that will end soon. Think about why you're grateful for x.

Stop Overthinking & Develop Healthy Coping Strategies - Both overthinking and negative life events can lead to a cascade of negative emotions. And since you can't experience positive and negative emotions at the same time, both of them can keep you from experiencing happiness.

Distract Yourself - This is the easiest, most underrated, and most overlooked strategy to deal with overthinking. Instead of getting completely absorbed by the negative ruminations of your mind, simply redirect your full attention somewhere else — watch something that's fun, call a friend, exercise, or do the laundry. The key is to pick a distraction that fully absorbs your attention so that you don't have the opportunity to lapse back into ruminating.

Distracting yourself helps give you some much needed space and perspective. Chances are you will realize that whatever you were ruminating about wasn't that bad after all. The mind is a master manipulator that can lull us into some worst case scenario and make us feel as if the whole world is falling apart. If you distract yourself early enough, you can stop the mind from getting too much momentum.

Write it Down - Writing down your worries helps you disconnect from them. When you see your thoughts on a piece of paper, you start seeing them for what they are: just thoughts floating in your consciousness. Once on the paper, your mind automatically let's go and you stop taking your worries so seriously.

Next time you catch yourself worrying, or ruminating, why not just write it all down (digitally or on a piece of paper) for ten to twenty minutes? If it makes you feel better, great! You've just discovered a new way to deal with overthinking if it doesn't work then there's no harm done. Just give it a shot.

Label Negative Emotions - Research has shown that merely labeling an emotion is enough to reduce its impact. The reason this works is that labeling something requires you to bring the prefrontal cortex online – which automatically cools down the brain regions responsible for emotion processing.

So, next time you're feeling bad, ask yourself, "What am I feeling exactly? Is it anger? Sadness? Fear? Shame? Guilt?" Then, simply describe the emotion in a word or two. Don't obsess over it – a word or two is more than enough. And then go about your business.

Practice Forgiveness - Holding on to negative emotions about a person who wronged you stops you from feeling happy and hurts *you* more than anyone else. Forgiveness helps you let go of your grudges, creates beautiful emotions of compassion and understanding, and helps you become a happier and more peaceful person.

Here's the gist of it: People, you and me included, are puppets of their conditioning. They are born innocent children and then get conditioned by the environment they grow up in. This conditioning or programming is what makes all of our decisions. We believe we have free will (it certainly feels that way), but our brain (the conditioning) makes the decisions before we're even aware of it.

The kind of programming you and I end up with is random. We can't be held responsible for our unconscious beliefs and value judgments. We were innocent children, who accepted the programming from our parents, teachers, and every other influence in our environment.

The point is: People don't hurt you on purpose. They just don't know any better, and just do what they think is best. They're just acting out their conditioning. It's nothing personal.

Go on a Brisk Walk - Take a 15 to 20-minute walk to notice as many pleasant things — sunshine, rain, silence, flowers, smiling strangers, light, birds tweeting, a cat walking across the street, wind stroking your arms, friends laughing together, two lovers holding hand, and so on — as possible to create an upbeat state of mind.

Research shows that this creates more happiness than merely taking a walk without deliberately trying to notice good things.

Act like a Happy Person - You become what you pretend to be. If you want to boost your happiness, start behaving like a happy person. If you look good, you feel good. If you feel good, you do well.

Smile More - Research shows that smiling – whether you're aware of it or not – makes you happier.

Simply follow Dale Carnegie's advice: "Whenever you go out-of-doors, draw the chin in, carry the crown of the head high, and fill the lungs to the utmost; drink in the sunshine; greet your friends with a smile, and put soul into every handclasp. Do not fear being misunderstood and do not waste a minute thinking about your enemies. Try to fix firmly in your mind what you would like to do; and then, without veering off direction you will move straight to the goal. Keep your mind on the splendid things you would like to do, and then you will find yourself seizing upon the opportunities that are required for the fulfillment of your desire." Copy the behaviors of happy people

Here's a list of all the little things happy people do differently. Just choose some of these strategies and enjoy your boost in happiness:

Practice Acts of Kindness - Randomly doing a good deed for one of your fellow human beings is a quick way to feel better about yourself and lastingly raise your level of happiness. It even makes you more successful in other areas of life.

Give the Gift of Time - Here's an interesting idea to practice kindness from Deepak Chopra. "One of the things I was taught as a child, and which I taught my children also, is never to go to anyone's house without bringing something — never visit anyone without bringing them a gift," he explains in *The Seven Spiritual Laws of Success*.

"You may say, 'How can I give to others when at the moment I don't have enough myself?' You can bring a try to find the perfect hotel to book, the perfect t-shirt to buy, the perfect place to sit on, the perfect outfit to wear, the perfect job to apply for, or the perfect movie to watch, you'll be unhappy for sure.

Realize that 99.9% of the time, good enough is good enough. Go through your life eating a good enough breakfast, getting a good enough cup of coffee, and maybe even a good enough life partner. You'll save a lot of time and you'll be a lot happier, too.

Create Anticipation - Anticipating a future event has a surprisingly large impact on your happiness. If you want to feel happier, make sure you put something exciting on your calendar that you can look forward to. Here are a few ideas:

- **Create plans for the weekend** - Just plan any kind of activity on the weekend that you can look forward to. Go hiking, visit a theatre, arrange a tennis match, go out for dinner with your spouse, plan a party, or whatever.

- **Plan a vacation for a few months or next year** - Mimic what the people did in the study from earlier: plan a vacation so that you'll anticipate it and enjoy a happiness boost for approximately eight weeks.

- **Make a plan to do something fun at the end of a hard day's work** - If you know at the beginning of your day that you'll have a lot of work to do, give yourself a little happiness boost by planning some fun activity at the end of the day. Maybe plan to watch a movie, go out for a drink, or enjoy some quality time with your girl- or boyfriend.

- **Spend Time with Nature** - Research shows that spending time in nature boosts your happiness as well as your physical, mental, and emotional well-being. The prescription is simple: whenever possible, go outside — even if it's just for a few minutes. And see the world around you.

- **Pursue Meaningful Life Goals** - Happy people have projects. If you want to experience a sense of hope and excitement about the future, you probably need to create some goals. As you think about potential future goals, keep the following guidelines in mind:

- **Focus on intrinsic, not extrinsic goals** - Intrinsic goals are the ones that satisfy your core needs for relatedness, competence, and autonomy. These are goals that are about making, supporting, and improving relationships. They are also goals that focus on personal growth, physical health, and self-acceptance — in other words, addressing your shortcomings or simply coming to terms with them. And they are about contributing to your friends or helping others fulfill these needs.

- **Make it specific -** If your goal is vague, it's too easy and too tempting to just take the easy way out when you're getting tired, bored, or otherwise discouraged. But there's just no fooling yourself if you're going after a specific goal. You've either achieved it or you haven't.

- **Make it difficult -** People do what is asked of them, and rarely more. Ask for a great performance and you're likely to get it (as long as you're specific about what great is!). By setting yourself a difficult goal, you're likely to rise to the challenge. It'll help you feel motivated and chances are you'll find yourself putting in a lot of effort, focus, and commitment. Following these guidelines helps you get the most happiness out of your goal pursuits.

- **Shock and Awe -** Awe is an emotion we experience when our typical way of seeing the world is challenged in a positive way. It involves the sensing presence of something greater than the self, along with reduced self-consciousness and a decreased focus on small, everyday concerns. Such experiences have been shown to expand people's perception of time and improve their well-being. Once you have an experience of awe in mind, describe it with as much detail as possible. Relive the experience and feel the sensation of awe take you over. Bask in those positive feelings for as long as you like.

- **Become a Lifetime Student of Happiness** - Research shows that merely learning about the subject of happiness can make us happier – a phenomenon I suggest has to do with priming and unconscious behavior activation. Whatever the exact reasons for why this works, I suggest becoming a lifetime student of happiness. Read books, watch videos etc.

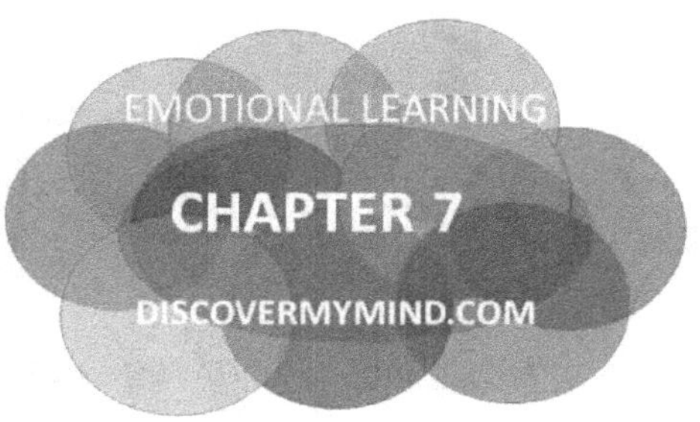

The DNA of Emotional Intelligence
LEARNING DOMAINS:

Learning is everywhere. We can learn mental skills, develop our attitudes and acquire new physical skills as we perform the activities of our daily living. These domains of learning can be categorized as cognitive, reflective and affective domains.

Cognitive Domain: (Learns well by understanding) involves the development of our mental skills and the acquisition of knowledge. The six categories under this domain are:

- **Knowledge:** the ability to recall data and/or information.

- **Comprehension:** the ability to understand the meaning of what is already known.

- **Application:** the ability to utilize an abstraction or to use knowledge in a new situation.

- **Analysis:** the ability to differentiate facts and

opinions.

- **Synthesis:** "the ability to integrate different elements or concepts in order to form a sound pattern or structure so a new meaning can be established.

- **Evaluation:** the ability to come up with judgments about the importance of concepts.

Affective Domain: (Learning by motivation) the affective domain involves our feelings, emotions and attitudes. This domain is categorized into five sub-domains, which include:

- **Receiving Phenomena:** the awareness of feelings and emotions as well as the ability to utilize selected attention. Example: Listening attentively to a friend.

- **Responding to Phenomena:** active participation of the learner. Example: Participating in a group discussion.

- **Valuing:** the ability to see the worth of something and express it. Example: An activist shares ideas on climate change.

- **Organization:** ability to prioritize value over another and create a unique value system. Example: A teenager spends more time online than with family and friends.

- **Characterization:** the ability to internalize values and let them control our behavior. Example: When we place our beliefs over our values.

Reflective Domain: (Learning by repetition) this psychomotor domain is comprised of utilizing motor skills and coordinating them. The seven categories under this include:

- o **Perception:** the ability to apply sensory information to motor activity. Example: A cook adjusts the heat of stove to achieve the right temperature for the dish.
- o **Set:** the readiness to act. Example: An obese person displays motivation in performing any planned exercise.
- o **Guided Response:** the ability to imitate a displayed behavior or to utilize trial and error. Example: A person follows the manual in operating a machine.
- o **Mechanism:** the ability to convert learned responses into habitual actions with proficiency and confidence. Example: Doing any task after understanding the tools or science behind it.
- o **Complex Overt Response:** the ability to skillfully perform complex patterns of actions. Example: Typing a report on a computer without looking at the keyboard.

o **Adaptation:** the ability to modify learned skills to meet special events. Example: A designer uses recycled material to create a dress.

Origination: creating new movement patterns to meet an objective. Example: A choreographer creates new dance routines for different music.

Again, many of us are unaware that the IQ remains relatively constant while it is the EQ that evolves and develops throughout our lifetime. And that we use only a fraction of our combined IQ and EQ on a regular basis. All emotions reside in our subconscious where 90% of our thoughts and actions originate. The rest are what is known as 'automatic thoughts' which are at the conscious level.

EQ is our emotional quotient which is about identifying emotions (in ourselves and others), relating to others and communicating our feelings. Our IQ on the other hand is our conscious self. Both can be measured through quantitative testing to evaluate intellectual capacity, like grade point averages and academic rankings, or the multiple intelligence discussed herein.

An Overview of All Emotions

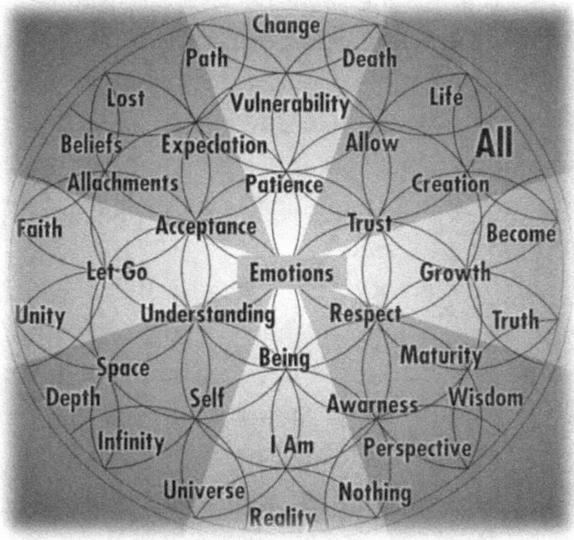

COMPONENTS OF OUR EMOTIONAL INTELLIGENCE

Emotions can be pleasant, beautiful, regrettable or painful. We must cherish all the positives, and not dwell on negatives, as they are of no use whatsoever.

1. Negative Emotions

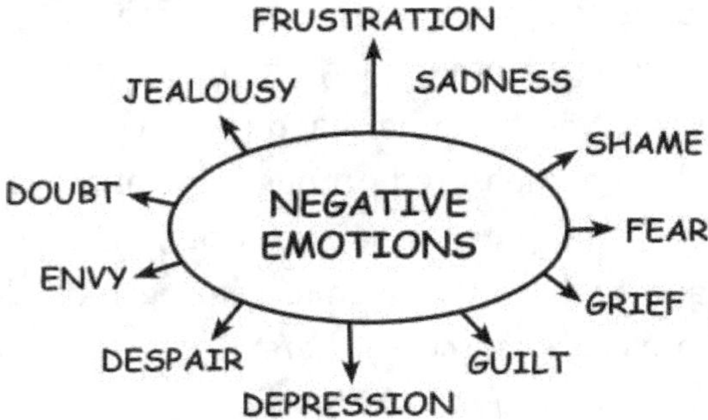

Emotions are the key driving forces around human existence, the fulcrum of our behavior, and the most powerful leveraging mechanism invented. Emotions and feelings surround us every day resulting many times in inexplicable action/ reaction. Emotional scars take a long to heal, and until that happens, love and trust are hard to restore.

Since our emotional baggage is filled with guilt, regret, angst, blame, remorse and recrimination, it often becomes too much to carry indefinitely. This needs to be resolved immediately or the 'excess baggage' charges will keep increasing. Emotions bring us to a two-way street where the ebb and flow between aggressor and aggrieved flow simultaneously but not equally, in both directions. Memories also play a crucial role as decisions are made based on the past and not the prospective future.

Fear - Fear is the insidious cartel formed between the holy grail of emotion and anger. We live in constant fear of what is going to happen in the future, what might come to be and sadly, what might have been. Fear and anger control the price we have to pay for our happiness. It is clear that together, they are the main incendiaries in human relationships. Social interaction, while this cartel is at work, is like fighting fire with more fuel. But we think we are too clever for ourselves and are sure that we will douse the blaze somehow, someday, and in some way. This is wishful thinking at its best.

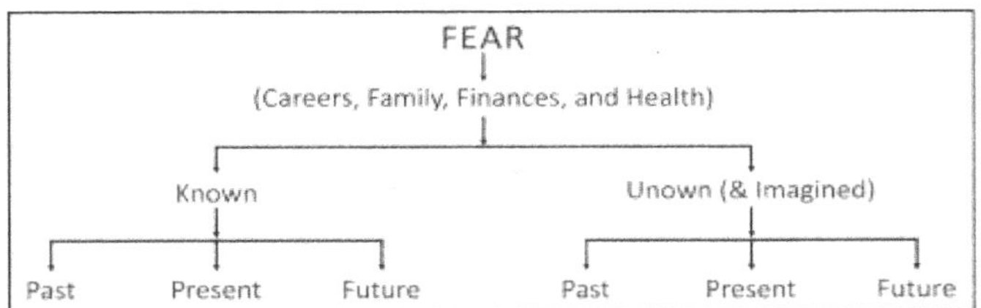

Another troika that forms is between relation-ships, honesty and trust. If unmanaged, this triangular collage many times unfolds with misunderstanding and misdirection.

What are the basic causes of fear and anger and how do we conquer each? These are difficult questions with many an answer. We try different approaches at different times with different PPE in order to arrive at our desired destination. However, unless we decipher the above and act on it resolutely and continually, it is next to impossible to move on. This is mainly because the above-mentioned cartel and troika paralyze us into not doing what otherwise is actionable. While emotions and anger are real, fear is imaginary and we must let go of it or it will disallow us to do that which we can and should do. This reminds me of a truism. 'Sometimes, today is the tomorrow we were worried about yesterday", and defines the very paradigms we face.

Survival - is our basic emotion. It involves:
- Instinct
- Desire
- Escapism
- Life situations
- Identification
- Discontent
- Attention
- Reality
- External world
- Compassion
- Compulsion
- Communication

- Wisdom
- Overthinking

Relationships - There are two types of relationships. The one we have with others and the one we have with ourselves. Therefore we should examine our motives before saying or doing anything since it determines what we or they do next. Unless our word or action is true, it's good and it helps, we must not say or do it. The other person's thoughts and feelings are more important as we cannot take them for granted. In any event, the end result of any situation before us is a direct function of the response we give or receive, for anything or from anyone.

'Great minds discuss ideas, average minds discuss events, and small minds discuss people' – Therefore we must resonate and connect with others and find areas of mutual interest even if we agree to disagree. We know what is going on within us but are reticent to share with anyone thinking they won't understand. What the truth is we really do not say. We are like candles in the wind and sharing our feelings with others is our best shelter. This is when the empathy, sympathy and compassion reach out and complement each other.

We should never disconnect with others nor judge them even if they judge us. Our attitudes, thoughts, and feelings determine ALL our actions, our lives, and in fact our entire being. Over the swirling currents of our many emotions, we must decide which bridges to cross and which ones to burn. For those we care about, we must re-connect. For the rest, we should walk away and let them be. When the evidence is indisputable and the verdict foregone, there is little room in the PPE courthouse to plead that we are the ones being misjudged or victimized.

We must know the difference between an honest debate and a fruitless argument. If the latter is not worth it, walk away. Sometimes silence may serve as an effective and alternate form of communication, but we must be careful when adopting this approach as it can sometimes be taken as a token of admission of guilt. Marital discord, with possible sexual dysfunction and alienation from family and friends, is the first casualties. If unchecked, divorce and estrangement are likely eventualities. It is important to understand that relationships cannot be restored or maintained without honest communication. In any discourse, it is imperative for us to know who, when, where, why, which, what, and how they are related to the issues at hand, and what is at stake. This thought-provoking process takes time to analyze but is worth it.

Our judgment of others is based on our own beliefs and value systems. The belief judgment says he or she has done 'it' once and will do it again. The value judgment says no, they are trying their best and will prevail. Therein lays the fragmentation of our approach toward our loved ones.

In order to understand our inner self, we must review the following sequence of events that occur, each morphing into the other sequentially: Memories- Thoughts- Disappointment- Helplessness- turning into Hopelessness- Altered emotions- Sadness- resulting in Resentment- Anxiety-Stress- Tension- Fear- Anger- Rage. These become the force behind our action and ultimately, reaction. Once we understand this evolution cycle, we will know how our ecosystem emerges and converges, and how to deal with it.

Games People Play- Almost everything we do in life is ultimately a game, from the mundane to the profound, and from a board game to the board room. We don so many 'masks', one above the other, to conceal our real identity. These masks have to be removed layer by layer to reveal who we are really are. Our world becomes a stage where we all begin playing clever roles waiting for the curtain to come down even before the play is over. It is a travesty that we become too clever, and fool ourselves in the process, particularly under peer pressure and difficult situations.

People play mind games in order to regain control of both sides of the fence. If we elicit a gratifying response from someone or if we get them to do what we want, it gives us a power buzz and makes us feel that we are in charge. Otherwise, we introverts.

We try to influence or 'manage' our lives in a variety of ways best suited to us. A mindset emerges. How can I outfox someone out of whatever it is I want. And the brain goes into overtime and overdrive. Sometimes we are oblivious to the play-action unfolding before our eyes. Whether it is us or related PPE, manipulation and exploitation become an art form, and emotions become a game with different players, strategies, and rules yielding unpredictable results. There are games we play thinking we are going to win, and those we don't because we are afraid to lose. Who really wins and who loses? This is anyone's guess but ultimately, it is only the outcome that matters. Because life in its totality is a game we cannot afford to lose and must win at all costs, without any game playing.

Game theory aside, people play games primarily to win. The main objective being is to get a 'high' from outsmarting, outwitting or convincing someone. The moves we make and the strategy we employ is a function of our desired objective, but ultimately it all depends on who holds the trump card. I hope the *entire* content of this book is viewed through this prism. Once we do this, reality emerges and it is insightful, fascinating and worth trying.

Emotional Acceptance - If we have let our emotions harm our loved ones, we need to understand and accept this misbehavior, get over it, deal with it and make amends. Examine what has been lost, what is left and how to regain some if not all. Situations that need to be thought through are the:

- Trust we have squandered.
- Love we have lost.
- Expectations we have decimated.
- Happiness we have abandoned.
- Respect we have discarded.
- Relationships we have disowned.
- Health we have suffered.
- Selfishness we have displayed.
- Careers we have destroyed.
- Finances we have squandered.
- The future we have compromised.
- The honesty we have eroded.
- The family we have sacrificed.
- The pain we have maximized.
- The soul we have minimized.

Fear & Anxiety - Fear is one of our most common and pervasive feeling and can affect our lives in countless ways. We need our fear at times to warn us of impending danger, but sometimes our fears play tricks on us and mark danger where none exists.

- Fear is our body's way of telling us to "Pay Attention".
- Fear can save our life (literally).
- Fear is in our heart (feelings), but it's fueled by our mind (thoughts).
- Fear is future-based. We fear what might or might not happen.
- Fear and l ove are the only 2 primary feelings.
- Fear can be debilitating.
- Fear can range from minor discomfort to a full-fledged panic attack that renders us incapable of functioning. Fear can make us freeze or fear can make us panic and run. It's our choice.
- Fear has probably ruined more lives than any other feeling, including anger. Fear can be very subtle and quiet, leading us to avoid, decline or bow out of life without us even noticing the impact. Beware of *"No thanks."* and *"I don't feel like it, today."*
- Some theorize that we are born with only two fears: fear of falling and fear of loud noises. This is good news because it means that all our other fears were learned (nature) and can therefore be unlearned.
- Choose an acronym that best suits you:

    ○ FEAR = "Flee Everything And Run" or

○ FEAR = "Face Everything And Recover"
- The opposite of fear is faith, and trust.
- Meet and beat your fear.
- Courage is not the absence of fear. Courage is being aware of your fear and pressing on, anyway.
- People will often do more to avoid the feeling of fear than to attain joy.

Anger - All anger is manufactured. We are not born with anger; we learn it as all of it. It is 100% based on our thoughts. There is no 'natural' anger as it is always optional. Always. Listen to your anger and it will tell you:
- Who you are.
- Who you are not.
- What you care about.
- Who you are afraid about.

- **Anger is a 'secondary' emotion.** We always feel something first, before we feel angry. For example, if we get angry at someone for cutting us off in traffic, notice that there was first a feeling of fear.

- Anger can be very manipulative. Some control others with their anger.

- **Anger is a wonderful tool** that was given to us to help if we use it wisely.

- If you don't know, appreciate and learn to like your anger. Do not deny your anger. Do not ask, "Am I angry?", instead ask, "What am I angry about?" It's in there. Find it. Use it. Make friends with it. Make sure you benefit from its power and message.

- If you're motivated in some way, there is probably some anger behind your driving force.

- Anger with hate vs. anger with love - Anger can be motivated by hatred, or love. Which will you choose?

o Anger usually has a strong judgmental component to it. Notice your judgment "I don't like that." and work with the thoughts that drive the anger to release your anger.

o The best way to deal with anger is to just **let yourself be angry** even for a minute. Growl, clench, roar, scream to bundle up all your anger and let it out of your body. Allow the energy and whatever sound, noise or feeling to come out of you.

- When practicing rage reduction (also known as anger management), you can feel your anger as deep as you can, but do not hurt anyone.

- Ask yourself, "What else am I angry about?!"

- **Don't 'lose control' of your anger.** Consciously escalate it until you can 'let go' of it. *Losing control* means losing charge. *Letting go* means you are still conscious and in charge, and can get yourself back in control (which is high EQ).

- Anger is a most misunderstood feeling. It destroys more relationships than any other, but can change the world in positive ways.

Depression – A critical phase of the emotional life cycle. We go into depression when we:

- Have not come to terms with our weaknesses.
- Are not wishing to learn or listen.
- Want immediate results from unreal expectations.
- Try to exercise control over the uncontrollable.
- Let emotions overwhelm us.
- Abandon our belief and value systems.
- Let false pride and prejudice prevail.
- Begin to judge others over ourselves.
- Depression causes the persistent feeling of sadness and/or loss of interest in things that were pleasing before and causes significant disability in functioning in daily life.
- Everyone feels upset or demotivated from time to time. Depression is more serious than just feeling sad and can be a mood disorder characterized by prolonged feelings of sadness and loss of interest.
- There can be a biological basis for depression that

requires medication. The emotional component to depression should also be addressed & relieved.

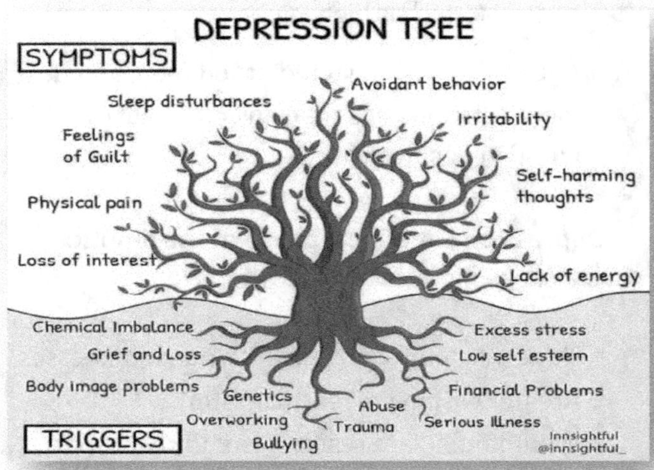

- Depression is feeling numb to emotions.

- Depression can engulf all our thoughts, and the world seems like a dark place, with no hope and no light. Other things which seemed interesting once now seem dull and hopeless.

- Depression is often a symptom and not an illness.

- According to the National Institute of Mental Health (NIMH), major depression is one of the most common mental disorders across the world.

- Depression can consist of persistent feelings of sadness, hopelessness, worthlessness, emptiness, irritability, frustration, restlessness, fatigue, and lack of energy.

- It may also hinder thinking clearly, remembering,

concentrating, or making decisions
- Appetite or weight changes
- Recurrent thoughts of death or suicide
- Physical symptoms such as headaches, stomach aches or back pain
- Experiencing some combination of these symptoms at least two weeks likely signifies that you are in the midst of a depressive episode.

Happiness - The 4 Levels of Happiness
- Level 1: Happiness from material objects.
- Level 2: Ego gratification. Happiness from comparison: being better, more admired than others.
- Level 3: The happiness from doing good for others and making the world a better place.
- Level 4: Sublime. Ultimate, fullness and perfect happiness.

Kinds of Happiness
- **Nature happiness:** This is the kind of joy that can be derived from the creation, the happiness we experience through our physical senses
- **Social happiness:** We find so much wonderful pleasure in our family and our friends.
- **Vocational happiness:** Although our jobs can often frustrate us. This is opposed to experiencing much

job satisfaction and even exhilaration when things go well.

- **Physical happiness:** The joy we have in being fit, strong and healthy, and being able to do what we want to do.

- **Intellectual happiness:** The pleasure that comes from understanding something – analyzing it, explaining it, improving it, remembering it and using it.

- **Humor happiness:** The enjoyment felt when you hear a good joke, strange irony or coincidence, or an unexpectedly positive event, especially with someone you like.

- **Spiritual happiness:** This joy often fills and even floods a believer's heart as he/she feels incredible faith, glory and hope.

By your decisions, you either decide to take action or decide not to. Consciously choosing puts you in control.

- Behind every action you take is at least one reaction.

- **'No action' is an action** and is often the wisest action when it comes to strong feelings and emotions (you can feel as much as you want/can/need to, without doing anything or saying anything to anybody.

- The key is to CHOOSE your actions and non-actions

knowingly, consciously, wisely, not reactively, unconsciously and/or habitually.

- **A major component of EQ:** The ability to think a thought or feel a feeling without having to act on it.

Personality refers to individual difference in characteristic patterns of thinking, feeling and behaving.

Inspiration - Whether from our PPE, the counselor or the environment, inspiration is our adrenalin. It jogs us out of our mundane daily routine and stimulates us into thinking positively. Of many a dictum or doctrine, inspiration is and has been the source of the greatest achievement in the world. We must find the source that can provide inspiration and hold on to it dearly, for it is the road to nirvana. It does not have to come from some extraordinary discovery; maybe just from our PPE, some happy news or a memorable event. And forgiveness by others does not necessarily mean what happened is O.K. and that you are welcome back in their lives unconditionally. It just means that they have made peace with the pain and are willing to let it go. This should apply to us as well.

Love - One of the most misunderstood words in the human lexicon is 'love'. There is more to it than we think. It is not without reason that the poets have eulogized it over centuries. But we have distorted it to mean something that it is not. The result is a struggle, disenchantment, and frustration. Love for most people is a means of fulfilling various needs. For professionals who build relationships with business partners and colleagues, the relationship is invariably related to economic survival. For those who invest in romantic relationships, the issues at stake are often sexual or psychological. People may claim that all these are founded on love. However, most are fundamentally   transactional and governed by vested interests.

The moment certain expectations are not fulfilled, love evaporates. Indeed, it is often replaced by hate or bitter disillusionment. The fundamental problem is that we human beings have based our lives on the fallacy that love involves another. Based on this limited understanding, we create a plethora of relationships. This may be a working arrangement for domestic purposes, but for those who seek more abiding well-being and freedom; this is a highly limited and impoverished idea of love. In actual fact, love has nothing to do with anyone else. Love is just the way you are. It needs no external stimulus and is entirely self-propelled. Love is simply a state of emotion. However, the compulsive nature of people's desires makes them eulogize love and freeze it into a set of limited, calculated & conditional transactions. To then extoll the virtues of 'unconditional love' is a gross travesty!

It is amazing how love works. If someone truly loves you, nothing you can do or say will deter them. In fact, they tend to see through your anguish and love you even more.

Honesty & Trust - Trust once lost, is like a broken piece of glass that can only be glued together, a thread once cut, that can be joined only by a knot, or a crumpled piece of paper that is impossible to straighten. Loss of trust, faith, and credibility is the casualty, along with the dishonesty that comes with it. It is possible though improbable to mend broken trust. It is almost impossible to mend a broken heart.

Building trust in ourselves is equally important and is an integral part of self-esteem discussed earlier. We should find the good in ourselves, something that was always there but had not surfaced before, and something we thought we had lost over time but was always there.

These are truth serums so potent they can overcome any adversity. They must be of the absolute kind in order to be of the permanent kind and are invaluable assets that, in their absence, no relationship can exist, survive or grow. There can be no love without honesty. All we need to say and what our loved ones want to hear, is the truth, the whole truth, and nothing but the truth.

We know the truth hurts. That is why we sometimes tell a 'white lie' in order not to offend someone. Or say, "I never lied; I just hid the truth." Even if these rationalizations are valid, they still aren't okay. Truth needs no justification or the need to be proven by anyone to anyone, about anything. Whatever we do or say must come from the heart and not the mind. There is a distinct differential here, one that should be noted by the observer. If we tell the truth it is a part of the past. If we tell a lie it becomes a part of the future. For some inexplicable reason, we just don't realize that we are lying to ourselves first before we lie to others.

Triggers - Each trigger is like a mental ignition device ready for combustion at the earliest, and arrive in packages small and large. They come into play in the formative, developing and recovery phases of emotional stress, cannot be anticipated or predicted, and will strike like lightning.

A sudden success or a dismal failure in any given instance is all it takes. Since our lives are full of conflicts and each is different, they form the basis for triggers to manifest. Conflicts cannot be resolved as and when they occur, but must be managed over time, and not be disowned or allowed to fester. Triggers are our Kryptonite (a la Superman). An effective way to negate triggers is to flash a picture of your loved ones in your mind, look at it for a minute and think about what they would say or do if you did what you were intending to do. Another is to keep busy with something that is productive so that the mind is occupied, or at a minimum diverted. This is to preclude our fertile imagination from looking for an unwanted outlet to dispense its inherent energy.

Enabling - Most family members and friends plant a sense of dependency in us to provide extra comfort, sometimes as a way of recompensing assumed deprivation. To all loved ones: beware of the sympathy card that is played with pleas and tears. Exploitation begins when someone enables us financially or emotionally to remain dependent and not come to terms with the problem, thus allowing the masquerade to continue. This is another case where one tries to find the appropriate balance between need and want. And deciding what to do or not do while at the same time trying to keep the overall objective of helping the aggrieved in mind.

Enabling can take many forms and usually results in

negative activities. Despite good intentions, enablers stand between conflict resolution and sympathy. This comprises well-wishers, friends and family members who unwittingly retard progress. When the enabling system turns into an intervening one, things get complicated and change for the worse.

Amends - Making amends is essential to the healing process and the only way to regain all aspects of a relationship. It is clear that unless we admit to the things we have done and convey them with honesty and sincerity there can be no reception to any overture or a chance of reconciliation. Calling or writing to the ones you care for most and saying, "Look, I'm sorry if I hurt you and wish to make it up to you," is step one. Then of course is proving we are doing everything possible to change and correct ourselves. It doesn't matter who or what started it. We must figure out what needs to be said, how, when and to whom. The longer we wait, the less is the impact and the more the jeopardy.

We cannot be concerned about the chances of success or how others will or did react, or what if they didn't or don't. Amends should be made without reciprocal expectations. If the changes in our personality and behavior are palpable, the relief and response we have been wanting and waiting for so long is assured. We should do this consistently and not as an occasional pursuit.

Making amends is much more than an apology. Taking responsibility for mistakes and repairing the harm done is one of the fundamental steps in behavior management. Nobody is perfect and humans constantly evolve and are bound inevitably to make mistakes. Stumbling blocks help mold our character which is built from experiences. And there is no shame in admitting we were wrong.

Habits - We must change our habits to change ourselves. The first is self-knowledge or knowing ourselves. At times, a single idea can change the habits of a lifetime, in a moment. Like smoking or drinking. Trying to do this in moderation rarely succeeds, and it is better to do it once and for all. Another way is to change our surroundings as they are main influencers. We must be clear what we want to change, and when we see the results we should reward ourselves appropriately.

We have heard the refrain – "I am sick and tired of being sick and tired. I give up"! Please don't. Or we will eventually rise to the highest level of our incompetence. Giving up and giving in are self-imposed, self-perpetuated and erroneous assumptions and doing so without really trying is not acceptable. There is a difference between giving up, knowing when you have had enough and not giving in. Never say it can't be done or I can't take it anymore. It has, can, should and will be done. This affirmation must be a part of any planning we do.

Pain - Pain is a major cause and outcome of emotional distress, either physical or mental. In the latter context, it is caused by and results from one or more of the following:
- An unsatisfied ego.
- A lack of acceptance of the way things are.
- Unfulfilled expectations.
- Anger.
- Frustration.
- Disappointment
- Relationships.
- Emotions.
- Feelings.
- Memories.
- Fear.
- Our PPE

We think that pain is something accidental just happens and will ultimately go away. Not so. Pain can be temporary, recurring, pervasive or permanent. Sometimes we hold on to it forever. A sad memory, something someone said, did, or didn't, or a broken promise. Almost anything can induce pain. Like fear, pain can be real or imaginary, troubling and disruptive. We sometimes compare our pain with that of others. If their pain is greater, we feel elated. If our pain exceeds that of others, we get depressed. We then use medication, drugs or alcohol to minimize or subdue the same, only worsening it. Pain comes from unfulfilled desire or expectations and inability to avoid the inevitable. It comes not from actual privations or insults but from thinking how it all could have been avoided. Ultimately, it is all about how we manage and mitigate this key symptom of depression.

Trauma - The term trauma is usually been associated with physical injury but has implications in our emotional health as well. It is damage to the psyche that occurs due to severely distressing events caused during childhood or adolescence. Trauma also results in anxiety or fear linked to emotional or psychological stress. Unfortunately, there is no real cure for past events or experiences that can be removed.

Whenever possible, please stop, think carefully and take the time to analyze present relationships. For each of the following, identify the status for and in any given problem situation. The:

- **W**ho
- **W**hen
- **W**hat
- **W**here
- **W**hy
- **W**hich and
- **H**ow

Doing this will assist and result in rational and appropriate decision making.

Identity - Sometimes we experience a loss of identity, which comprises our character, reputation, beliefs, values and personality. Most of our identity is established during adolescence and does not change much except our own interpretation of it, which then becomes the reference point for our thoughts and emotions for the rest of our life.

Ego - An interesting aspect of ego is that it possesses meaning and self-expression, which people understand but do not necessarily accept. It is a manifestation of our state of mind where personal considerations are first and foremost, otherwise known as selfishness. We convince ourselves we are not the problem but the solution, blame others, shirk responsibility, get angry, resentful, belligerent, and decide to take action only when we realize we are in the wrong. Ego is simply our 'self' immortalized and has the power to make or break our personality depending on how it is demonstrated. Ego is a bottomless pit that can never be filled no matter what. It is like a one-way mirror looking inward only.

Here are some lessons we can take in 'ego management'.

- o Get in touch with our own true self - This means time taken to look deep down into our being, free the mind from worries and be in the present.
- o Be impartial and not easily offended - There will always be something or someone bothering us, so don't let it get to you. Just let go and walk away.
- o Don't look for victories in arguments, or wish to be noticed or even look better by comparison. Learn not to be a winner always & never judge others.
- o Be content with whatever we have.
- o Be a kind and gentle person in every way possible.
- o Stop delaying your world or it will spin out of control.

Denial - Denial is the ability to convince ourselves that we are the victimized soul, and not otherwise. It consists of lying, obfuscation, deception, dishonesty, apathy, lack of sympathy, empathy, and disrespect; along with other traits that lead to moral bankruptcy.

A misdirected angst emerges. One simply cannot proceed in life without overcoming this ultimate form of self-deception and undesirable behavior. The sad part is that it is WE who choose to be in denial. Warnings from family members, friends, employers, and even doctors are ignored or rejected. We enter a world of our own, become inaccessible to others, and derive satisfaction from being self-righteous. In doing so, a blame game, finger-pointing, and guilt-tripping ensues. We also stop caring and show no appreciation. We simply have to overcome this major obstacle and accept reality.

Self-pity & Self-esteem - Self-pity is imaginary, self-induced, assumed, contrived, self-deprecating, contagious, and a form of self-harm. It worsens the mental state leading to paranoia and a sense of abject failure that may even induce suicidal tendencies. Things we didn't say, do, or could and should have done continue to haunt us. Instead of being despondent, we need to get a grip on ourselves and not be deterred by naysayers. We sometimes feel we have good reasons to feel sorry for ourselves, but indulging in such thinking is risky and a waste of time. The inspirational Helen Keller once claimed, "Self-pity is our worst enemy. And if we yield to it we can never do anything wise in this world".

We need to write down our list of resentments, whatever they are or maybe. The key lies in overcoming this 'feeling', because our thoughts are in our control. Self-pity is just a disruptive mechanism that must be disabled to let the mind revert to its original self. Negativity brings down our mental immune system and only a strong dose of internal and external stimuli can salvage us from this dangerous frame of mind. Self-esteem is inversely proportional to external control and self-pity. Part of the hard to define variables of the emotional equation is that we know what the constants are such as love, trust, and honesty, but variables such as fear and anger are moving targets that are hard to pin down.

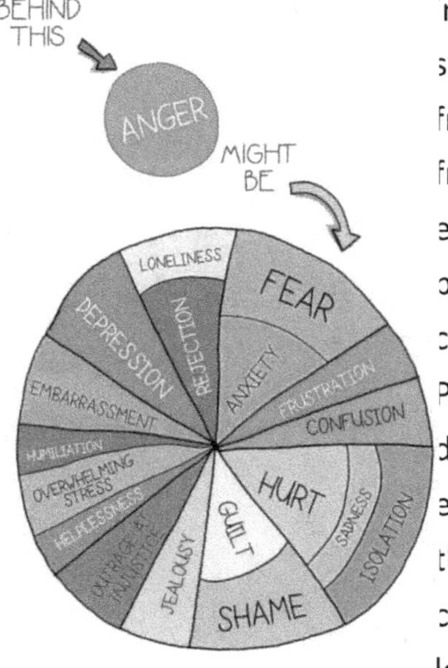

Our consciousness is 'volitional' and not living mindfully creates a diminished sense of self-worth and self-respect. We cannot feel competent and worthy while our thoughts are in disarray. Furthermore, we establish the kind of person we are through the many choices we make, between thinking and non-thinking, and being unaware of reality or evading it.

Knowing - Every human being we meet in life knows something we don't. And inside every person we think we know, there is something we don't. The worst feeling is when someone we know becomes someone we knew. We should forgive ourselves for what we did not know, were doing, but know better now. We are the only ones that truly know who we are because no one else does.

Self-reflection and evaluation raises many questions. They are or could be:
• To confirm what we know
• To know what we don't know
• To hear what we want to hear
• To judge others' opinions
• To disrupt dialog for lack of attention
This is an example of how our mind works when understanding and responding to each other. Most questions are not trivial and no answer is

meaningless.

The brilliant French psychoanalyst, Jacques Lacan taught us, 'anger results as a psychological defense against threats of fragmentation.' Anger affects how we feel, think and behave. It becomes symptomatic through our reactions to things around us and by our own thoughts and worries or those of others. We are more likely to be angrier when we do not know how to control it.

Social interaction with someone who cares is an effective way and can calm down our nervous system in anger. Someone we can connect with personally and who will listen without judging or criticizing and give the attention required.

Anger is the punishment we give ourselves for someone else's mistake. We are often silent when we are screaming inside. If we don't understand why someone else is silent, we cannot expect them to listen to what we have to say.

Anger is directly proportional to fear and hence to emotion. That is why working on our fears helps bring down anger. We tend to internalize anger and resentment and have been angry at everything and everyone for so long because things went wrong. Meeting someone with whom we can share what's on our minds will be a welcome relief. Expressing our feelings and seeing if he understands who or what is bothering us will be heartwarming. Any latent energy bottled up inside us is of no use, now or in the future. Tolerance and temperance coupled with patience is the key to anger management. They are the hardest things to adopt because ego and emotions are always in play.

Levity - Many EI literacy programs do not proactively include humor as an integral part of their curriculum. The ability to laugh at oneself, share, and to listen to others is important, can change our entire outlook and how we begin to perceive each other. A funny joke, a hearty laugh, a happy smile, a pat on the back, or sharing memories of hilarious moments makes a world of a difference to our outlook and has underestimated therapeutic value.

Loneliness - Family and friends don't know what is going on deep inside each one of us. Neither sees the tears or feels the pain on the other side. More so, loneliness occurs when we stop connecting with others.

The best advice is to ensure we have around us people we can share our thoughts, problems and future. After all, no one can be an island unto themselves. People who are social wannabes will go to extremes to overcome their loneliness. Lonely people prefer to stay this way and create a shield that is difficult to penetrate. That is why loneliness can be ascribed as a prime trigger, and why the company of others is an essential antidote.

Keep in mind that loneliness isn't the same as being alone. That is why it is possible to feel lonely even when we are among others. Sharing experiences and feelings is another way of changing the situation. This includes feedback and advice. Sometimes we feel there is no one to turn to. When this becomes a chronic problem, drugs or alcohol tend to provide temporary relief, are not the real answer and can lead to despair and depression.

Addiction - The mind is where it began and where it will never end. We live in our mind that is made of self-awareness, emotions, motives, desires and thoughts and our every action and reaction is a direct result thereof. Addiction leads to self-deception, detachment and insensitivity, resulting in behavior that is not only morally reprehensible but beyond comprehension. Even a drunk derelict will surprise us with something thought provoking, unexpected and profound. Like, "Hey, if there is no wine in Heaven, then I'm not going"! This is because the subconscious is still functional while the conscious is disoriented and numb. The alcoholic brain is always looking for wrong solutions, in the wrong places, at the wrong time with the wrong methods, yet expecting the right result.

> "Whether we accept it or not, almost everyone is an addict. From the mild to the severe, of some persuasion or another, to some degree or another, for some reason or another and with some consequence or another. This is not only the inconvenient truth, but a fact of life".

Our PPE are a major source of inspiration and influence us. Many people are deeply motivated by the accomplishments of successful people, make them role models, and emulate them. Conversely, if we subscribe to bad influencers, we let their behavior change ours and we lose control of our own thoughts or reactions.

The basic soul-searching question we keep asking are things like what went wrong, why did this happen, who am I, what did I do, and what do I do to get out of this mess. These keep echoing in our minds and make us impatient for answers. After overcoming denial, the first step in finding answers is to remove the cobwebs that are in our minds and identify the changes needed in our entire way of life.

People say fate and destiny cannot be changed! Yes, there are some things we cannot change like gravity, the speed of light or potential energy. But there IS one thing we can change, and that is our attitude and behavior toward   ourselves and others.

Personality Attributes:
- Dominant
- Influential
- Realistic
- Compliant
- Investigative
- Conventional
- Artistic
- Enterprising
- Social.

Personality type is our behavior in learning, execution, and communication. Primary personality is when we are actively, dynamically responding to external stimuli (e.g. stress). Secondary personality is our behavior pattern when we are relaxed or when there are no external stimuli. The five major personality types are:

COGNITIVE : (DOMINATING TYPE)
- Autonomous, very strong-willed, independent, likes to lead others.
- Tends to analyze, classify, test, apply & research

- Enjoys debate and research, and get into explaining the theory of a matter.
- Has the courage to pursue goals, keep promises, and pursue fairness and justice.
- Concerned about self-image, enjoy winning, lack in-depth communication.

- Unable to adapt in an environment of high stress.

Due to the type of education and environmental influence after birth, goal-oriented people can be divided into (1) Goal-oriented (Entrepreneur Type) and (2) Goal- oriented (Research Type).

Recommendations for Self-improvement:
- To be more caring, more encouraging, empathetic so that others feel appreciated.
- Try to get involved in communication skills such as listening skills and the ability to resolve disputes.
- Embrace an open-minded attitude, and not pay attention to unwanted criticism during work.

- Pay more attention to the merits of others.
- Avoid setting unachievable pars and benchmarks and expect others to achieve the same.

INTEGRATIVE (Diplomatic type):
- Can integrate resources and information.
- Can have multi-perspective thinking.

- Adapts to new things, ideas and concepts easily in order to achieve goals.
- Have excellent resilience, patience and perseverance. Plan new things with goal-orientation, sometimes with more than one goal or idea.

Recommendations for self-improvement:

o Work plan should be drawn up in advance, practice good time management, learn to prioritize work according to importance and urgency.

o Plan for the future. Encourage the self to continuously learn and grow. Achieve goals one at a time.

o Empower others.

o Maintain the consistency of principles and not change benchmarks.

o Become an expert in our own expertise and avoid being a jack of all trades.

o Adopt self-analytical strategy (e.g. SWOT analysis).

AFFECTIVE (Flexible Type):

- Enjoys group activities & tend to listen to others opinions.
- Is not easily affected by our own emotions, or people and situations.
- Is not dominant, complies with the rules of the game and goes with the flow.
- Enjoys being at ease and dislikes being restricted.

- Resents working hard or alone for a long period.

Recommendations for Self-improvement:
o Learn to be dominant and control the work flow. Participate in decision-making and goal setting.
o Do macro thinking & demand achievable outcomes from self & others.
o Take part in various community activities and take the initiative to try and be the leader.
o Read autobiographies of successful people & books on time management and learn how to increase efficiency.
o Try and record encouraging and self-affirming words. And reject bad advice and people.

REFLECTIVE (Obedient Type):
- Are simple, like to do familiar work, down-to-earth & realistic.
- Dislike theories, abstract concepts, over-complicated instructions and matters that serve no practical use.
- Are usually more conservative and have difficulty in expressing their own views, and require immediate feedbacks.
- Enjoy hands on activities; require demonstrations, training and concrete outcomes.
- Easily molded during adolescence, but lack self-study capability. Prefer to do routine and trivial work.

Recommendations for Self-improvement:

o Read more in order to feed the sponge-like desire for knowledge.

o Do not refuse to do work because it is trivial (b) Don't be defeated by failure (c) set targets & train own self to be persistent and efficient (d) reduce the tendency to retreat (e) Don't make excuses and give up or give in.

o Find own strengths, place emphasis on in-depth learning of skills or content.

CRITICAL (Challenging Type):

Our way of thinking often differs from others. The main aspiration that drives us is our interest in whatever makes our lives happier. We like to ask questions, and are persistent in getting the answers which we will evaluate critically. We are self-centered and prefer to look at things in a different way thus people tend to regard us as eccentric, peculiar, rebellious and remote. We have a rather high acuity and as a result are able to make quick decisions without lengthy considerations.

- Are creative, and very competitive.
- Thrive on setting new standards and challenges.
- Are influenced by reverse reasoning and use reverse psychology
- Use stages and points accumulation to achieve rewards

- Motivated by challenges and use self-planning and self- management

Control - There are many things inside of us that we can control and many, many things outside of us we cannot. Know the difference. Manage what you can and let go of the rest.

There is perhaps no more empowering belief than understanding that you're always in control of how you feel. Control can be an illusion since it is often ego-based; yet it can be one of our biggest motivators.

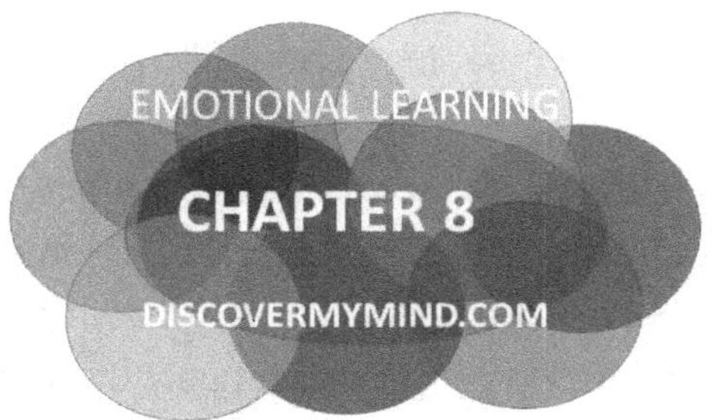

Spirituality and the Cosmic Equilibrium

Our SQ or spiritual quotient is a combination of things in the inner self, be they value or belief systems, morals or ethics, and comprise all aspects of the human cosmos.

It is worthwhile noting that spirituality helps in developing tools needed for reflection and emancipation. Spirituality is based on beliefs of inner strength and moral values. Although associated with religious beliefs, it represents a broader, non-denominational interest and does not require attendance in a religious place of worship. For many, spirituality is defined simply through the actual experience of:

- Heightened awareness.
- Acute clarity.
- Feelings of understanding and empathy.
- Authenticity and self-validation.
- Increased sense of meaning and purpose in life.
- Seeking forgiveness from others.

- Attributing meaning to one's life experiences

While the dictionary defines spirituality as 'relating to a person's spirit', or 'relating to a person's religion or religious beliefs about God or the soul', in reality, it is perceived differently and subjectively by each person, as we all have a different meaning and purpose in life.

Spirituality is an underestimated application in behavior modification by the medical profession at large but has now gained worldwide acceptance. This technique gives our nervous system deeper levels of rest such that the memories of stress themselves begin to lose their hold over us. This is partly because we are now producing all the right number of neurotransmitters and hormones, which are nourishing every part of our being. Also because our corresponding receptor sites can recalibrate to a more accurate level of sensitivity, and can be cleansed of any pharmacological debris.

Living Consciously - means to seek and be aware of things that have a bearing on:

- Our actions
- Our purpose
- Our values and
- Our goals

How we behave is by what we see and know. Living consciously also implies regard for our needs, wants, likes, and dislikes to our inner and outer world.

Specifics of Living Consciously

- Being 'in the moment' and not agonizing about the past or worrying about the future.
- Searching for feedback from the environment and adjusting or correcting our course as necessary.
- Re-examining old assumptions, i.e. what we think we already know.
- Being interested and open to new information or ideas as they can change our plans, decisions and direction.
- Being willing to see and correct our mistakes.
- When we tie our self-esteem to our errors and omissions we shrink our consciousness by engaging in self-protection.

Meditation also results in greater activation of the prefrontal cortex, which makes us more rational and less recklessly impulsive, making it easier to make good decisions and avoid the path of least resistance.

It also washes out the emotional charge of environmental triggers that otherwise cause us to use.

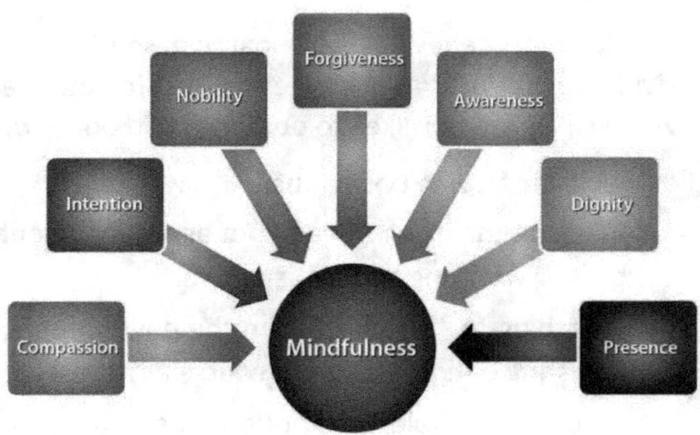

We know how a powerful smell can reawaken a long-forgotten memory. Well, that is exactly what happens when we are faced with a trigger the body remembers as being intimately related to a big success or failure. For all these reasons we begin to see why meditation is a great preventer of depression. Further, emotional intelligence can ultimately be viewed as a state of consciousness to help develop our nervous system and nourish our being.

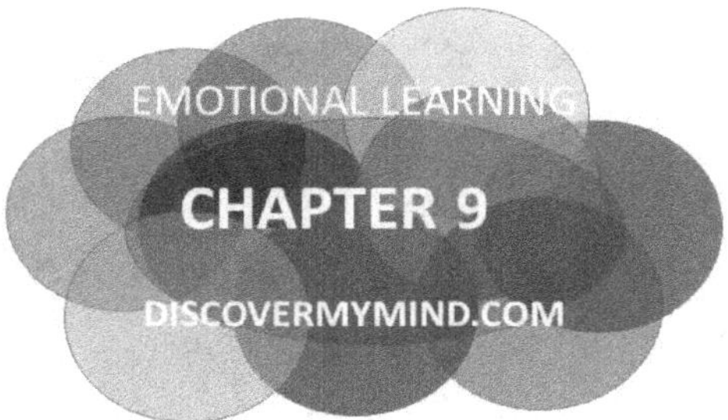

Personal Profiling and Assessment
Measure What Matters

Since emotions are subjective, creating accurate, reliable, quantifiable, repeatable, statistically-viable testing can be difficult. However, due to its importance and popularity, some numerous tools and instruments attempt to properly measure and assess EQ.

Testing modalities include:

- Rating of emotional skills and competencies

- Facial expression recognition

- Situation understanding and decision-making

- Emotional vocabulary

- How emotions are identified and processed

- 'Other reporting', often called '360s', which ask others above, below or beside you to rate how well they believe you handle yourself and your emotions.

What is the need of Intelligence Profiling and Assessment?

○   Identify the best learning style for him/her.

○   Identify his/her inborn talents and weaknesses.

○   Tailor-make learning programs.

○   Assist in subject and educational stream selection

○   Improve relationships between parents and children

○   Develop self-confidence.

Parents often face questions like: - Why is a child's emotional health the key to academic success? What is the difference between IQ and EQ? How can I enhance the learning abilities of my child? How can my child achieve their maximum potential?

For answers to these and other related questions, and if you find your child is becoming unmanageable, avail the assistance of an EQ profiling and assessment test. This detailed assessment from a certified psychologist becomes the basis for clinical guidance needed and is a road map for career planning. Thousands of students and parents in other countries have benefited from this approach, and this is now being implemented in knowledge-driven societies like India.

Encourage taking a profiling and assessment test.

This is an easy, inexpensive test done in complete privacy. It analyzes the in-born multiple intelligence, strengths, and learning disabilities, and provides a clear road map for further intervention as may be needed. Thousands of people have taken this test worldwide which has resulted in a significant improvement in academic or career performance.

An EQ assessment is important in achieving scholastic success. It will:

- Enable the parent to understand how their child thinks, learns and understands.

- Identify the personal thinking preferences so that learning can be tailored to achieve that goal.

- Contribute to the student's happiness and self-esteem.

- Provide insight into the what, how and why of the student's behavior, and to manage it with empathy and compassion.

- Establish much needed communication and restore relationships.

- Make the right subject and career choices.

- Deal effectively with stress and anxiety and in some cases, depression.

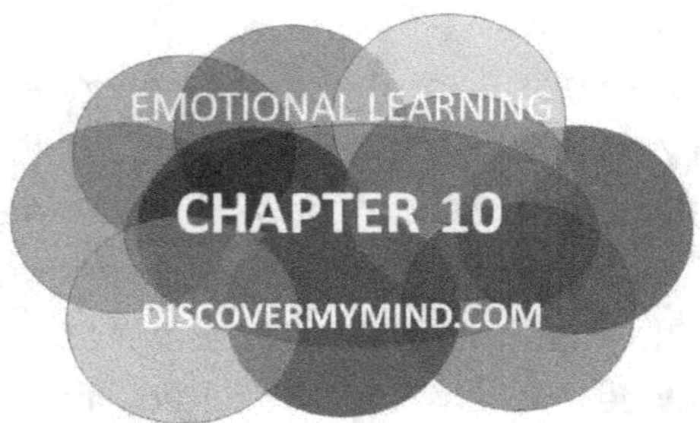

Parenting and Counseling

5 Emotion Coaching Steps for Parents

1. Tune in to your child's feelings and your own.
- Pay attention to your own emotions, from happiness to sadness to anger.
- Understand that emotions are a natural and valuable part of life.
- Observe, listen and learn how your child expresses different emotions at different times and in different ways.
- Watch for changes in facial expressions, body language, posture and tone of voice.
2. **Connect with your child.** Use emotional moments as opportunities to connect.
- Pay close attention to your child's emotions and try not to dismiss or avoid them.
- See emotional moments as opportunities for teaching.
- Recognize feelings and encourage your child to talk about his or her emotions.
- Provide guidance and solutions before emotions

escalate into misbehavior.

3. **Listen to your child.** Respect your child's feelings by taking time to listen carefully.

- Take your child's emotions seriously.
- Show your child that you understand what he or she is feeling,
- Avoid, *"I know exactly how you feel."* as you can only guess and approximate.
- Avoid judging or criticizing your child's emotions.

4. **Name emotions.** Help your child identify, name and separate different emotions.

- Identify the emotions your child is experiencing instead of telling your child how he or she is feeling or should feel.
- Naming emotions can help soothe your child.
- Set a good example by naming your own emotions and talking about them.
- Help your child build a vocabulary for different feelings.

5. **Find good solutions.** Explore solutions to problems together.

- Redirect misbehaving children for what they do, not what they feel.
- When children misbehave, help them identify the thoughts and feelings they had prior to the action, and explain why their behavior was inappropriate.
- Encourage emotional expression, but set clear limits on behavior.

- Help children think through possible solutions and expand their choices.
- Don't expect too much too soon emotionally, but be persistent and continue focusing on feelings over time.
- Be aware of tempting settings, emotional triggers and be prepared to help your child them.
- Create situations where your child can explore without hearing lots of "don'ts."
- Acknowledge when your child is doing things right and praise him/her. "Caught you being good."
- Do chores, like picking up toys, together.
- Make tasks as fun as possible, yet successfully get the job done.

The 5 P's of Parenting

Be Patient. The frustration will pass but this will be your child for the rest of your life.

Be the Parent. Your child will find and develop friends. But he or she desperately needs a parent.

Be Practical. Your expectations and demands should challenge but not exceed your child's ability.

Be Positive. Your child will strive to fulfill your words, good or bad.

Be Protective. Your child needs a safe haven in this troubled world; let it be you.

Raising an Emotionally Intelligent Child

- **Focus on strengths**. When your child brings home a test, talk first about what he or she did well. Then talk about what can be improved. Praise specific strengths. Don't just criticize things that were done wrong.

- **Follow up with consequences for misbehavior.** Sometimes parents say things in anger that don't curb the behavior in the long run. You might say, "Because of what you did, no television for a month." Both you and your child know that after one or two days the TV will go back on. Decide on consequences that are fair, and then carry them out.

- **Ask children how they feel.** When you ask your child about his or her feelings, the message is that feelings matter and you care.

- **Find ways to stay calm when angry**. It's normal to get angry or irritated sometimes. Learn to recognize "trigger situations" and do something about them before you lose control. Try taking deep breaths for a few moments. Consider having a "quiet area" where people can go when they are upset. Or you can just stop talking and leave the room for a while. Sit down as a family and talk about what everyone can do to stay calm.

- **Avoid humiliating or mocking your child**. This can make children feel bad about self. It can lead to a lack of self-confidence and, in turn, problems with schoolwork, illness, and trouble getting along with friends. Unfair criticism and sarcasm also hurts the bond of trust between children and parents. Be mindful of how you speak to your children. Give them the room to make mistakes as they learn new skills.

- **Be willing to apologize.** Parents need to be able to apologize to their children if what they said was not what they meant. Calmly explain what you really wanted to say. By doing this you're being a good role model. You're showing how important it is to apologize after hurting someone. You're teaching that it's possible to work through problems with respect for the other person.

- **Give children choices and respect their wishes.** When children have a chance to make choices, they learn how to solve problems. If you make all their choices for them, they'll never learn this key skill. Giving children ways to express preferences and make decisions shows that their ideas and feelings matter.

- **Ask questions that help children solve problems on their own**. When parents hear their child has a problem, it's tempting to step in and take over. But this can harm a child's ability to find solutions on his or her own. A helpful approach is to ask good questions. Examples include, "What do you think you can do in this situation?" and "If you choose a particular solution, what will be the consequences of that choice?"

- **Read books and stories together.** Reading stories aloud is a way to share something enjoyable and learn together about other people. For example, stories can be a way to explore how people deal with common issues, like making or losing friends or handling conflicts. Ask your child's teacher or a librarian to recommend stories on themes that interest you and your children.

- **Encourage sharing and helping.** There are many ways to do this. Together you and your child can prepare food in a homeless shelter or go on a fund-raising walk-a- thon. You can help out elderly neighbors or needy families. This teaches children that what they do can make a difference in the lives of others.

Tips to Raise Caring, Confident, Capable   Children
By working together, schools and parents can promote children's social and emotional learning (SEL). SEL includes:

➢ **Self-awareness**—recognizing feelings and managing anger.

➢ **Understanding others**—developing empathy and taking the perspective of others.

➢ **Making responsible decisions and following**

through. This includes considering long-term consequences of your actions for yourself and others.

➢ **Understanding yourself** —handling emotions, setting goals, and dealing with obstacles.

➢ **Building healthy relationships**—saying no to negative peer pressure and working to resolve conflicts constructively.

➢ When youngsters master these skills, they are more likely to succeed in school and life. They become happier and more confident. They are better students, family members, friends, and workers. They are less prone to drug and alcohol use, depression, or violence. Social and emotional learning is like an insurance policy for a healthy, positive, successful life.

➢ **The Role of Parents** Long before children can say their first word or take their first step, they respond to the touch, tone of voice, and moods of their parents. This is the beginning of learning about emotions and relationships. It happens as naturally as their bodies grow and develop.

➢ "Family life is our first school for emotional learning," states author Daniel Goleman. In the family, he says, "we learn how to feel about ourselves and how others will react to our feelings." This learning happens both through what parents say and do to their children and how they treat each other.

- ➢ **Children learn important lessons about emotions from their parents.** When parents threaten or punish children for a display of emotion, children learn emotions are dangerous, to be held inside. This can lead in later life to depression or unchecked rage. When parents do not teach their children acceptable ways to express anger, the children may think it is okay to strike out at others or have tantrums.
- ➢ **Parents should think of themselves as "emotion coaches."** They can encourage their children to use feeling words, such as "I feel sad" or "That made me really angry" to express emotions.
- ➢ **When children learn to express feelings and respect others, they become happier and healthier.** Such children are less likely to have problems with depression, violence, or other mental health issues as they grow older.
- ➢ **Many SEL programs for schools include activities for parents.** When parents and students practice SEL skills at home, the effects are even greater. Students also come to see learning as a lifelong process, not something that stops when they leave school.
- ➢ **Children want their parents to guide and teach them.** A recent poll found that 86% of young people 10- 17 years old said their parents were very important influences on their lives. Only 22% said television, movies, and popular music were so important. No one can take the place of parents.

Counseling - In counseling, communication is of utmost importance, including active listening, and allowing reflection and effective questioning to build rapport. The Counselor should be empathetic, see things from the person's viewpoint and not be too sympathetic i.e. feeling sorry. It is necessary to have sustained and expert guidance for serious behavior modification to be effective. A good counselor is someone who empathizes and inspires, whom we can believe in and who will provide a shoulder to cry on as an outlet for pent up emotions.

In counseling it is not the input or output that matters; it is the outcome. Both parties must be willing, tolerant and patient. And in life, it is not what someone asks anyone to do. It is what is followed up by each that matters. Depending on the person, counseling can be like trying to restrain the proverbial bull in a china shop. Periodic performance monitoring, health check-ups and counselor meetings are important checks and balances, and a means for program and progress evaluation. Impact assessments that measure improvements in lifestyle, social and professional outlook, temperament, decision-making and relationships are recommended. It is important to set measurable short, medium and long-term goals pertaining to all PPE, as each metric is achieved. Family counseling too is essential as it is the cornerstone of the support and feedback mechanism.

A counselor simply shows us where to place the troubling pieces in order to complete the behavior puzzle. The key to any counseling is not in the selling of the benefits but in the formation of a relationship with the person in a way that he or she will buy 'into' the concept.

Counseling is the provision of professional assistance and guidance in resolving personal or psychological problems. It comprises the act of helping the patient to see things more clearly and possibly from all viewpoints. This will enable both to focus on feelings, experiences, or behavior with the goal of facilitating positive change. Confidentiality is advised as it is a relationship of trust between two people.

Counselors are aware that no two people are alike and their understanding of the patient is linked to a specific experience. By talking openly and sharing freely in a way that is rarely possible with family or friends, who are likely to get emotional and have opinions and biases that may be detrimental to the process. It is important that the counselor is not emotionally involved with the person. He or she should neither judge nor offer advice unless essential, thus giving the client the opportunity to easily express difficult feelings such as anger, resentment, guilt, and fear. The counselor encourages the client to examine previous parts of their lives that were or now are difficult or impossible to face. Exploration of early childhood experiences throws light on why an individual reacts or responds in certain ways today.

Depending on the circumstance, the manner of questioning should be:

- Open ended and general in nature.
- Intellectually engaging.
- Informative, i.e. did you know that?
- Reflective, i.e. ideas, dreams, thoughts.
- Directly supportive, i.e. appreciative of the progress achieved.
- Emotionally supportive, with empathy and compassion.
- Interesting and thought provoking enough to raise new questions for follow up.

For the person interviewed, ensure that:

- They are happy and healthy both mentally and physically.
- They eat and sleep well.
- They think positively.
- They perform productively
- They accept responsibility.
- They are willing to take prudent risks. Failure is the best way to learn.
- They spend time with family and friends and are

not left alone.
- They control their thoughts and actions.
- They do not fall into bad habits or bad company.
- They have a good attitude about people, places and events.
- They succeed on their own merits.
- They respect their parents, teachers and curriculum.
- They don't give up and give in when things go wrong.
- They live in the present and not the past or the future.
- Make sure their core beliefs and values are exemplary.
- Make sure they have clear goals and re-evaluate them periodically.

Post-Counseling Intervention

Convincing someone to do something they are unwilling or unable to do can be frustrating and painful. The recourse is appropriate and proportional intervention. This is required for any effort in behavior modification.

There are six types of intervention based on the personality, condition and relationship with the patient.

- Indirect Intervention: thru loved ones.

- Direct Intervention: with loved ones and a Counselor.
- Forced Intervention: carried out by the Counselor with consent from the family.
- Confrontational Intervention: by confronting the person directly and informing them that the situation is no longer acceptable or tolerable.
- Crisis Intervention: in the event of suicidal, mental or severe physical illness.
- Relationship Intervention: with friends, family, and loved ones.

EQ for Teachers

Teachers must learn SEL before teaching it.

Training teachers to teach SEL can be tricky because SEL is not just another subject that can be taught from a cognitive-based textbook. Attempts at providing rote curriculum and lessons for teachers to present has only had mixed success. What has worked well is for teachers to first learn SEL/EQ on their own, incorporate it into their lives and then work these concepts and teachings into all subjects and most everything they do. There are many training and certification programs available to meet this requirement.

PART II

AN INDEPTH ANALYSIS OF CONCEPTS FROM
Part I

EMOTIONAL INTELLIGENCE - A MACRO VIEW

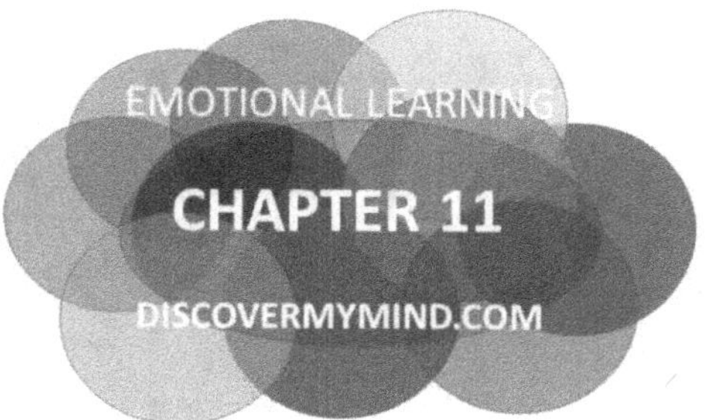

Multiple Intelligence

KEY FEATURES OF MULTIPLE INTELLIGENCE THEORY

1. Intelligence is a biological and psychological potential.
2. There are multiple and independent intelligences.
3. Intelligences always interact with one another.
4. Each person has a unique intelligence profile.
5. Intelligences are educable;they change and grow.
6. Intelligences can be learned throughout life.

Components:

- Critical thinking
- Cognitive thinking
- Affective Thinking
- Reflective Thinking
- Reverse thinking.

It is interesting to note the different forms of intelligence we possess, each having its own DNA. They are:

- Intellectual
- Spiritual
- Cognitive
- Intuitive
- Relative (emotional and social)
- Inherent (skills and knowledge).

And the new pursuit Artificial Intelligence, which only computer geeks understand but can seldom explain!

Our I.Q. or Intelligence Quotient, and E.Q. our Emotional Quotient, are not proportional. People with high I.Q. have an elevated sense of thought and perception and are able to rationalize and decide what to do quickly. On the other hand, those with high E.Q. respond swiftly to P.P.E. (People, Places, and Events) but do not exercise the same caution. When the two combine, awareness about all and sundry is heightened exponentially and is an ideal situation. Dr. Jeanne Segal, Author, defines emotional intelligence as "the ability to recognize, direct and positively express emotions". Emotions can override thoughts, transform relationships and profoundly influence behavior. A high EQ allows us to harness the power to understand ourselves, overcome challenges and maintain strong relationships.

It is said that men are from Mars and women from Venus. Our spiritual quotient notwithstanding, the intelligence and emotional quotients of men and women are very dissimilar and require different attention. This is something that many EI coaches and trainers fail to differentiate or incorporate in their programs.

All forms of intelligence and knowledge, when employed wisely and productively are the only assets in life that are guaranteed to increase in value the more we share them. They also form the cognitive framework needed to deal with when attempting behavior modification.

Our multiple intelligence is based on the following attributes:

- Verbal/Linguistic

- Logical/Mathematical

- Visual/Spatial

- Musical/Rhythmic

- Bodily/Kinesthetic

- Interpersonal

- Intrapersonal

Verbal/Linguistic - the ability to read, write, and

communicate, the ability to use language to express one's thoughts and to understand other people orally or in writing with words. It is learnt best by reading, taking notes, listening to lectures, discussion and debate. This intelligence is high in *writers, lawyers, philosophers, journalists, politicians and teachers.*

Logical/Mathematical - the ability to reason and calculate and employ abstract reasoning; also to manipulate numbers, quantities, operations etc. Many scientists, mathematicians, engineers, doctors and economists function with this type of intelligence.

Visual/Spatial - The ability to think in pictures, imagining things, visualize future results, perceive spatial information etc. People with strong spatial intelligence are proficient in graphics and images. This intelligence is high in artists, photographers, pilots, painters and architects.

Musical/Rhythmic - The ability to create, communicate and understand meanings made out of sound, the ability to compose music, to sing, and to keep rhythm, and the ability to hear music, tones, and larger musical patterns. Since there is a strong auditory component to this intelligence, we learn best by using songs or rhythms to learn and memorize information. Careers which suit those with this intelligence include instrumentalists, singers, conductors and composers.

Bodily/Kinesthetic - Allows individuals to use all or

part of one's bodies to create products, solve problems, or present ideas and emotions; using the body in highly differentiated ways for expressive, recreational, or goal-directed purposes. People who have this intelligence usually enjoy acting or performing and in general, are good at building and making things. Careers that suit those with this intelligence include athletes, dancers, actors, surgeons, and professionals.

Interpersonal-Social Intelligence – Enables individuals to recognize and make distinctions among others' feelings and intentions. The ability to work effectively with others and display empathy. Careers that suit those with this intelligence include business owners, managers, teachers, and social workers.

Intrapersonal - The ability to distinguish among an individual's feelings, to accurate mental models of themselves, and use them to make life decisions. The capacity to know one's self. Careers that suit those with this intelligence include philosophers, writers, psychologists, theologians, and scientists.

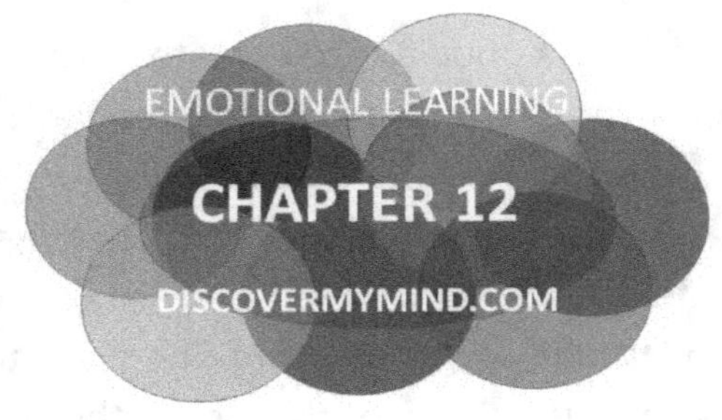

Social Emotional Learning (SEL)

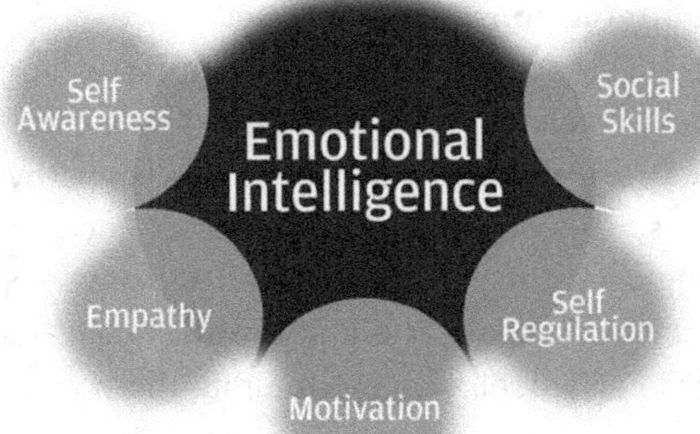

Identifying   Emotions

The ability to accurately recognize emotions is the most basic EI skill. The better the emotional read we have on a situation, the more appropriately we can respond to it. It is difficult if not impossible to recover from unreliable emotional data, and basing our actions on incorrect information is a recipe for disaster. We need to be aware of our feelings and those of others. Being aware of others' emotions is critical to building a successful workplace environment and quality interpersonal relationships. Imagine what it would be like to work with a colleague or be in a romantic relationship with someone oblivious to your feelings – never noticing them, never asking about them, and vice versa.

Using Emotions to Facilitate Thought

How we feel influences how we think. Using or generating emotions is to know which moods are best for different situations, and "how to get in the right mood." More specifically, this skill allows us to employ our feelings to enhance the cognitive system (thinking) and as such can be harnessed for more effective problem-solving, reasoning and decision-making. Of course, cognition can be disrupted by extreme negative emotions such as anxiety and fear, but emotions can be prioritized so that the cognitive system can attend to what is important and focus on what does best in a particular circumstance. For example, if we are feeling sad, we may view the world one way, while if we feel happy we will interpret the same events differently. Indeed, research shows that people in a sad or negative mood tend to focus on details and search for errors, whereas those in a more positive mood are better at generating new ideas and novel solutions to the problem.

Socio-Emotional Learning or SEL is a unique subject different than most. It is not rocket science or especially complicated, in fact, many of the concepts and lessons are surprisingly simple. Yet, there is much to understand, learn, practice and master. Dealing with our emotions can be painful and difficult. Yet SEL/EQ is arguably one of the biggest advances in mental health in many years, as it impacts every human being on many levels throughout our life, from cradle to grave. Our never-ending stream of consciousness changes over time and no two people think, feel and act the same way.

EQ and its importance - First, let's start with a simple self-reporting quiz, to see how you currently handle your emotions. It is helpful to know where to start by establishing a baseline to measure against. Take the quiz now and then take it again after reading the book, and see if any changes in your thinking have occurred.

How well do you manage your Feelings and Emotions?

Here is a 7-question, self-reporting, self-scoring quiz to determine your basic level of emotional agility.

Instructions: Rate yourself between 1 and 5 on each of the following questions, using this scale.

1: Not at all! | 2: Not well | 3: So-so | 4: Mostly good | 5: Yes, I'm excellent at that!

1. **Awareness-** When your body feels something (fear, anger, sadness, shame, guilt, etc.), how well do you notice and become aware of your feelings? 1 2 3 4 5

2. **Acceptance -** Is it Ok with you when you feel mad, or sad, or afraid? How well do you accept ownership of your feelings vs. judging, denying or blaming them on others?   1 2 3 4 5

3. **Identification -** When you notice that you're feeling something, how well can you identify the feeling you are having? How well can you separate and name your feelings correctly (for example, fear vs. anger)? 1 2 3 4 5

4. **Expression -** How well do you express your feelings and let them out of your body, as opposed to stuffing them down or bottling them up inside? 1 2 3 4 5

5. **Release -** Once your body feels a negative, unpleasant feeling, how well can you let go of that feeling and let it dissipate? 1 2 3 4 5

6. **Replace -** How skilled are you at replacing your 'negative' feelings (anger, sadness, fear) with 'positives' (love, joy, peace)? 1 2 3 4 5

7. Rejoice!

How well do you encourage and respect your true feelings, complimenting yourself for your awareness, expression and release?

1   2   3   4   5

Scoring Add up your 7 answers here:

Results If your score was between:

25-35   *High EQ*

Well done! You are quite aware of what's happening inside you, emotionally, and how to deal with it all. Where did you learn your emotional skills? With high emotional awareness, you probably feel quite happy with yourself, you are probably successful in most areas of your life, and your relationships are probably plentiful and satisfying. Congratulations.

15-24   *Median EQ*

You still have plenty to learn about yourself and your emotions. Without emotional training there could be a whole world inside you that you may not be fully aware of nor have access to. Do some work in this area and you will find more meaning, fire and depth to your life.

> *0-14*   *Low EQ*
>
> Please read on and continue your journey into SEL/EQ. It's likely to change your outlook, improve your results, and may even extend your life.
>
> **Reflect** What do you think and feel about the score you received? How will you use the awareness of your rating to better yourself in the future?

High EQ vs. Low EQ

Many talk about feelings in abstract ways, yet they haven't cried in years. That is not high EQ. High EQ is when we have 24x7 access directly to all our emotions. We become aware of them and can 'navigate' through them in effective ways or fight, deny and run from them. When you are sad, let yourself cry. When you feel angry, decide to express yourself (or not) powerfully, genuinely, and fully in an appropriate, intelligent, relationship-building manner. With high EQ, we can evaluate our thoughts, our belief systems, and even our past childhood to determine why we feel what we feel, the way we do and what triggers us. Better yet, by knowing ourselves well enough and having re-trained our thoughts thoroughly, we will rarely get agitated or angry at all.

● EQ is the study of you, me and us.

Meta-cognition: Awareness and understanding of

one's own thought processes. What we think about.

Meta-emotion: an organized and structured set of emotions and cognitions, both our own and those of others. Becoming aware of how we feel about things happening daily.

- **EQ is a set of highly teachable skills that reside in each of us from birth.** While our IQ is fairly static over time, we can make significant improvements in our EQ quickly, profoundly and often permanently.

- **EQ is completely free, natural and organic inside us.** We have the capacity and the capability, and only need to learn how to use what we already possess.

- **EQ is one of the keys to happiness, positive mental health and success in life.** Using simple, time-tested tools, knowledge and communication, we can become aware of, accept and take action to create or correct our own behavior, so it works for us and not against us.

- **EQ is a lifestyle choice.** We can live our life from a purely cognitive viewpoint, or we can add emotions to our cognition and incorporate all other aspects of our mind, heart and body.

Benefits of EQ

- **EQ can be the most relevant and practical subject there is.** EQ is 'always on' and functioning 24x 7x 365, every second of every day for the rest of our days. Whether we are aware of it or not, and consciously managing our thoughts & feelings or not.

- EQ can give us more control over our inner world than we probably ever thought possible.

- **EQ gives us the power to manage our own life.** No matter what happens outside of us, we have the ability to understand, manage and control what happens inside of us.

- **EQ is a skill set**, with happiness as the goal.

- **With EQ,** we can transform our negative thoughts and feelings into positive ones. We can replace and transform negative energy; severe painful emotions brought on by long-standing trauma from our past, and consciously replace them with love and happiness, in the present and in the future.

- **EQ gives us the freedom to choose.** Happiness is a choice: With EQ, we can learn to choose wisely.

- **EQ gives us the ability to respond rather than react.** Be an actor, not a reactor. A reactor is a victim and externally controlled by what other people do and/or say.

Not us. Because *life is 10% what happens to us, and*

90% how we react to it.

- **EQ can help make us stronger emotionally.** With EQ, we can build internal strength and courage, self- acceptance, self-esteem, self-responsibility and self- control.

- **EQ helps build relationships.** Once we learn how to deal with our negative emotions, we have the ability to reach out, and connect with people, 'risk' friendships and love relationships, and live a fuller life, knowing that, if things don't go well, we will be able to deal with any feelings of loss, rejection, disappointment and even depression, and still press on. (aka Grit)
Self-Awareness, Self-Acceptance, Self-Discipline

= lead to =

Self-Trust, Self-Motivation, Self-Confidence, Self-Esteem Self-Love and Self-Mastery

- **EQ can give us purpose, personal value and meaning to life.** If you know what you are feeling, you will know who you are and what you want.

- **EQ can teach us how to live a positive, productive, connected and empowered life.** Once we face, understand and 'conquer' our deepest, darkest emotions, we will no longer be afraid of our feelings. If we learn how to face, manage and master our own fear, anger and sadness, there isn't much life can throw at us that we won't be able to handle.

- **EQ affects all timeframes: past, present and future.** We can learn much from our past, live powerfully and fully in the present and create the very best future we can for ourselves and those we love. **EQ not only teaches us knowledge, but wisdom.** And not only how to manage information but also the practical application of that information in order to improve our lives positively.

- **EQ can help us heal our past.** Sadness, anger and pain can live in our brain, body and spirit throughout our lives unless we take the time and energy to find, acknowledge and release the same.

- With EQ, we can become fully engaged in our own lives and the lives of those we care about.

EQ is a win-win-win proposition. The more we know and practice EQ, the more everyone wins.

5 Key Skills in the Emotional Intelligence/ EQ Framework

There are skills, sub-skills and abilities under each component (below) that contribute to higher emotional intelligence, greater success as an individual, workmate and society member. These are:

Self-Awareness.

- Self-Awareness: Emotional awareness: recognizing

one's emotions and their effects

- Accurate self-assessment: knowing one's strengths and limits

- Self-confidence: sureness about one's self-worth and capabilities

Self-Regulation
- Self-control: managing disruptive emotions and impulses
- Trustworthiness: maintaining standards of honesty and integrity
- Conscientiousness: taking responsibility for personal performance
- Adaptability: flexibility in handling change
- Innovation: being comfortable with and open to novel ideas and new information

Self-Motivation
- Achievement drive: striving to improve or meet a standard of excellence
- Commitment: aligning with the goals of group or organization
- Initiative: readiness to act on opportunities
- Optimism: persistence in pursuing goals despite obstacles and setbacks

Empathy/Social Awareness

- Empathy: sensing others' feelings and perspective

and taking an active interest in their concerns

- Service orientation: anticipating, recognizing and meeting others' needs

- Developing others: sensing what others need in order to develop and bolstering their abilities

- Leveraging diversity: cultivating opportunities through diversity.

- Political awareness: reading   emotional currents and   power relationships at work or school

Social Skills

- Influence: wielding effective tactics for persuasion

- Communication: sending clear and convincing messages

- Leadership: inspiring and guiding groups & people

- Change catalyst: initiating or managing change

- Conflict management: negotiating and resolving disagreements

- Building bonds: nurturing instrumental relationships

- Collaboration and cooperation: working with others toward shared goals

- Team capabilities: creating group synergy in

pursuing collective goals

We are good at our IQ (intellectual quotient), but need to raise our EQ, emotional quotient to match and exceed. We are IQ heavy, and must make EQ the higher denominator.

Rational Mind + Emotional Mind = Wise Mind

Our school education has been primarily focused on our intellectual/cognitive IQ. We learn facts, knowledge and concepts, so we can get top grades and a career, but emotional health is by far more important for academic success.

Basic Truths We Should Know About SEL/EQ
- We are part of the human race with all that entails both positive and negative.
- Humans interpret the world around us through our senses and common sense. Yes! We all experience life differently than others, and every person's perspective or emotional lens is different.
- Humans have the ability to feel, sense, perceive and communicate at higher levels of consciousness.
- SEL & EQ offer skills that when embraced and practiced well, can help us navigate complex social and emotional milieu, and lessen or counteract possible negative behavior.

> • A benefit of embracing and practicing SEL and EQ
> skills is a higher level of understanding,
> transcendence, acceptance, empathy, self-
> efficacy, positive relationships, patience and love,
> to name a few.

Emotional Ignorance: Emotional education is not taught in most schools nor encouraged at home or work.

Since we get little or no formal emotional training, we have to figure it out on our own, as in the 'schools of hard knocks. Most parents didn't/ don't know much about EQ so they couldn't teach or show their children. We cannot teach what we do not know. So they did the best they could to 'cope' with the situation and often applied their thoughts and feelings poorly, providing a less than a desirable role model.

Over the years, the lack of emotional education by society   has contributed to consequences in several areas:

- **Personal Issues:** Like unresolved anger, long-standing grief, victim-mentality, low self-esteem, high levels of stress and anxiety, depression, inability to manage and control emotions, addictions, lack of self-discipline, repetitive failures, suicide, low levels of love, respect and joy, lower earning potential and a shorter lifespan.

- **Interpersonal Issues:** Ineffective communication skills, misunderstanding, dysfunctional relationships, lack of intimacy, abuse, divorce, domestic violence, child/spouse/elder abuse, rejection, and abandonment.

The good news is that emotional intelligence is now growing rapidly in importance and validity in all areas of life, as people are finding out how important and how powerful EQ   can be.

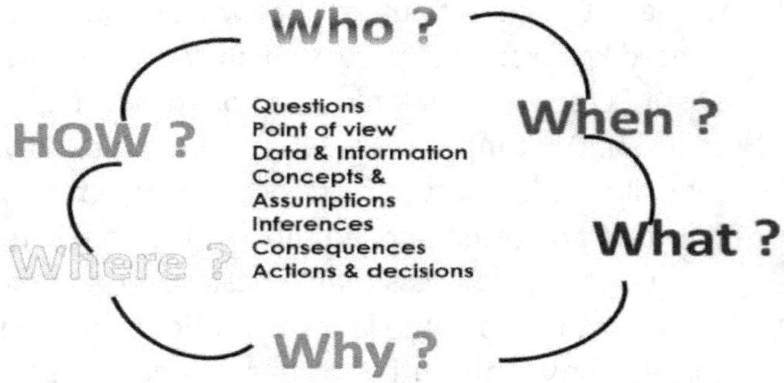

'Emotional Intelligence', 'EQ', 'SEL' and 'mindfulness' are becoming more mainstream, household terms.

SEL is being taught in many more public and private schools at all levels, from pre-school to PhD, partially by legislative mandate and largely due to teacher, school administration and parent demand.

0 At the end of 2020, about three quarters of schools in the U.S. now offer some form of SEL/EQ

education to students of all ages.

The high return on investment (ROI) of EQ training and support for customer service, employee engagement and retention and leadership at work demonstrates the cost/benefits of EQ practices in companies, agencies, and organizations everywhere.

According to the World Economic Forum, "Emotional Intelligence" is listed in the Top 10 job skills identified as 'must have' skills for 2020 and 2025.

With the growth in artificial intelligence (AI), there is an even greater need for an emotionally aware workforce.

Life is not about waiting for the storm to pass ... it's about learning how to dance in the rain!
~ Vivian Greene

Emotional Superpowers

- The bottom line is that EQ can give us what some are calling 'Emotional Superpowers', as they have such a profound impact on our lives and the lives of those around us. Powerful traits of EQ can include: Internal, personal and business relationships, Self-Awareness, Self-Acceptance, Self-Esteem, Self-Motivation, Self-Control, Resilience, Perseverance Tolerance, Trust, Faith, Hope, Personal Power, Peace, Serenity, Compassion, Empathy, Joy, Love, Emotional Agility, Connection, Collaboration, Friendship, Family, Cooperation, Inclusion.... and more.

- The practice of EQ can be some of the hardest, most painful work we will ever do. Experiencing and learning from our fear, anger, sadness or pain can be daunting. Please be aware that:

- Emotions can be painful, are anger-inducing, can bring up childhood memories that were bottled up and stored inside us. Emotions can be confusing, non-specific and ever-changing.

- Emotions can also be used for ulterior motives, to manipulate and control and /or to take and not give.

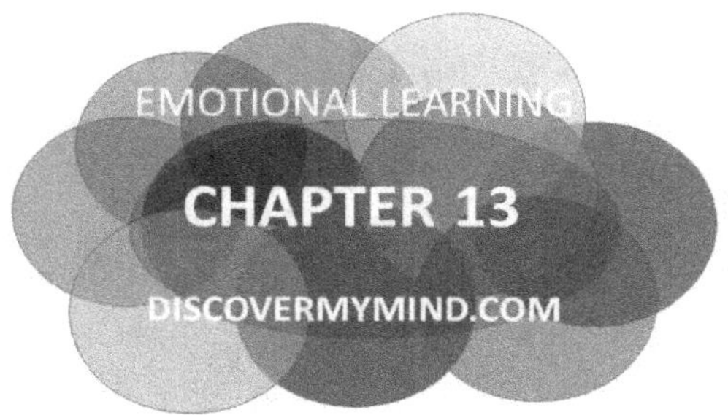

The Neuroscience of Emotions

The mind controls all five sensory and motor organs. It is the faculty of attention, concentration, consciousness, perception, thinking, reasoning, judgment, learning, memory, and rational interaction. It is also the reflection of the soul or inner conscience and governs our entire being.

Our minds are constantly taking in all kinds of information from our environment and storing it, even unimportant things. When ideas are repeated often enough and with consistency, we form beliefs or generalizations, and these then affect the way we perceive reality and the way we behave. The inputs that support beliefs are called "reference experiences". The only way to change these beliefs, once they're solidly entrenched, is to either use powerful counter references that can't be ignored or applied consistently and with enough repetition, the same way the original belief was formed.

There are millions of neurons floating around in our brain. When different chemical substances are introduced by the brain, the neurons 'connect' to form a chain, which becomes permanent and stronger with a prolonged stimulus. Once this chain is established, it is hard to break and can only be reformatted or reprogrammed. This is called CBT.

From all the input we get, our mind pays particular attention to experiences that cause an emotional response. Our brain constructs a physical association or 'link' between the stimuli and the response so that in the future the same or similar set of stimuli will produce the same response. The stronger the emotion is, the stronger is the link.

Also, future experiences reinforce the link or even strengthen it. This effect is called 'conditioning' or 'anchoring'.

The mind will motivate us both to seek experiences that give us pleasure, and avoid experiences that cause pain; though it will do more to avoid pain than to gain pleasure. That's why bad habits are so hard to break. Though the long-term goal is to provide pleasure, if there is enough pain in the short-term our brain will 'sabotage' us.

Furthermore, the mind is usually motivating us to do what it believes best for us based on our current beliefs and anchors, even though it might contradict our conscious goals. This sabotage is called 'secondary gain'. Facts and information is the realm of our conscious mind. Our subconscious, however, works on imagery, symbols, and metaphors, and knows no objective reality. We have to work with our subconscious to change our generalizations and anchors; the rest will come naturally.

Our brain is always taking in information and processing it. Our thoughts are an integral part of this input. When we go over an experience in our mind, we get the same emotional response as when it happened. It is called 'reinforcement'. We can tell the difference consciously, but our subconscious processes and stores it along with everything else.

Our thoughts are powerful tools for change; it's just that we have been underestimating and underutilizing them until now.

The key components of brain dominance are:
- Focus and attention
- Analytical powers
- Memory
- Concentration
- Energy
- Attitude
- Language ability
- Emotional sensitivity
- Communication skills
- Power of expression
- Problem solving ability
- Decision making
- Motor skills
- Inborn Intelligence
- Logic
- Visualization

The EQ Lifecycle: Cradle to Grave –
Thoughts and feelings have a distinct scientific, biological basis within our human body, encompassing the brain, heart and nervous system. Our thoughts and feelings serve us well in a variety of ways, including protection, information gathering, an early warning system, direction, intuition and expression. All our other fears and anger are the result of our beliefs, values, expectations and conclusions we arrive at. These can be learned, unlearned and relearned.

We take in information via our five senses - sight, sound, smell, touch and taste. This information leads to thoughts and feelings that need to be channelized

When feelings go up, logic goes down; feelings take over resulting in actions and reactions.

Choices - One of the greater benefits of EQ is our freedom and ability to choose. Many people believe their thoughts and feelings are just 'who they are', and they have no control over them.

Not so. One of our most profound choices we have is choosing how much and with whom we open or close our heart as well as our mind to. EQ gives us choices that we may have ever thought possible before.

The key is to make our choices 'consciously'. When they are unconscious, habitual or based on childhood trauma, we are not in control.

When we make our decisions consciously we become 'at choice'. We don't need to be perfect but we do need to be aware of our imperfections so we can self- manage.

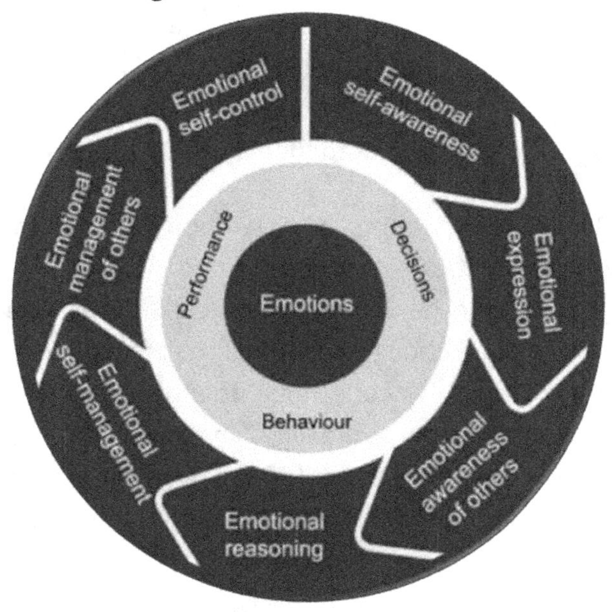

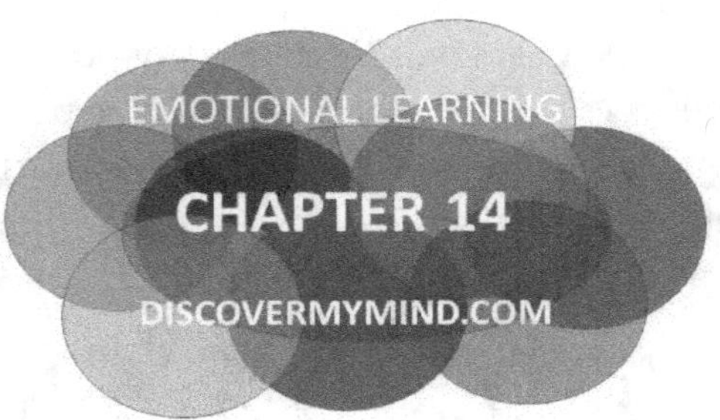

Components of EQ

The 3 Components of EQ: Thoughts, Feelings & Actions (TFA)

We need to be aware of and learn to manage and enjoy our thoughts, our feelings and our actions.

a. What we think - our thoughts and belief systems

b. What we feel - our feelings and emotions

c. How we decide to act (or not act) - our actions and behavior (or our inactions and non-behavior) lead to our outcomes and results.

3 Components of EQ: Think - Feel - Act

The key to EQ, and to taking control of our lives, is being able to effectively manage our TFA.

■ **Thoughts and Feelings are very different.** For the most part our thoughts originate in our logical left-brain (IQ), while our feelings come from our affective right- brain. It is helpful to learn to distinguish thoughts from feelings. For example: "I don't like you" and "you are bad news" are thoughts, while happiness and anger are feelings. Judgments and opinions are thoughts, while love, sadness, anger and joy are feelings.

- **We don't have to respond or react to all our thoughts and feelings.** They flow through our mind and heart, continuously and unending like waves in the ocean. We get to decide which ones we wish to surf.

- **Thoughts and Feelings are fleeting,** only the most important ones should be taken seriously and acted upon.

- **Thoughts become Feelings.** We (usually) have feelings first, then thoughts. If you think, "I'm safe and I belong here." you'll feel very differently than if you think, "I am unsafe and I must keep up my guard to protect myself."

- **Thoughts + Feelings become decisions, and our decisions become actions.** Every action, everything we do, say or write is based on at least one thought and one feeling. If we pay attention to both our thoughts and our feelings (IQ + EQ), then we are using all the important information our mind is trying to give us, so we can make optimally informed decisions.

- **Thoughts, feelings and actions are some of the only things we can truly control in life.** Luckily, they are the things we *need* to control in order to be happy, balanced and successful.

- **All three are critical.** Since they are the basic components of ourselves and our personality, it is essential that we learn as much as we can about how we think, feels and act.

- **All three are unstoppable and unavoidable.** We just cannot 'not think' and we cannot 'not feel'. We can try -- using distractions, drugs, and alcohol and so on to try to numb or depress them -- but we still think and feel, 24x7x365. Even if we are unaware, they still happen regardless.

- **All three are cyclical.** Thoughts create feelings which become actions. Our actions then elicit more thoughts, which create more feelings.

- **All three are changeable.** We get to choose.

- **Change one and all three change.** Since they're all connected, no matter which one you change, I all three will change accordingly.

- **Everything we do has a purpose**, or we would not do it. Right?

- **All three are teachable skills.** Each separately, and all three together can be improved and enhanced with knowledge, awareness and practice.

Thoughts - It all begins with our thoughts. They matter, a lot!

- **We get to choose our thoughts.** One of the most

critical components of EQ and one of the greatest gifts high EQ gives us is our freedom to choose what we think.

- **We may not be able to choose or 'control'** every thought we have, but we can choose which thoughts we want to ignore, replace the ones we don't like and are not working for us, and decide which ones to accentuate and embrace.

- **Thoughts are the key**! Our thoughts and feelings direct our decisions and actions & it's imperative we learn to manage them wisely:
- **Practice meta-cognition**. Notice, study and reflect about your thoughts.
- **Pay attention to your thoughts**, listen to them carefully and learn from them as you go.
- **Evaluate your thoughts** whether they are working for you or against you? Does that thought make you feel good or bad? Do you want to keep it or discard it? What is a better thought I could think, instead?
- If needed, adjust your thoughts - Remember, they work for you; you do not work for them.
- We are always free to think a different thought, to override a thought we don't want.
- Helpful stress vs. unhelpful stress is the difference in what you are thinking.

EMOTIONAL LEARNING

CHAPTER 15

DISCOVERMYMIND.COM

<u>Meaning & Belief Systems</u>

Let us talk about our belief systems, one of the most important components of EQ.

Belief systems are responsible for big, generalized, decisions we made in the past, usually as a child, to make sense of the world. The challenge is that some of our beliefs are unconscious, yet they often affect our current decisions, and run our lives on a daily basis *without our knowledge or permission.*

- **When something significant happens to or around us, we try to make sense of it and put a 'meaning' on it.** The event happened, but what did it mean to us? What did it mean to people around us?

- **Belief systems can be over-personalized.** Children are often great observers, but not good interpreters. When traumatic or severe things happen, especially events that involve our parents or other adults, we may see it accurately but we may interpret it incorrectly. People do things that have nothing to do with us, but we sometimes 'take it on' as if they were meant for us personally.

- **We like to be 'right',** so once we decide our actions; we often go through our lives unconsciously trying to 'prove' to ourselves that what we decided was/is true. As a teen or adult, we unconsciously create circumstances where we can say to ourselves, "See? I knew it."

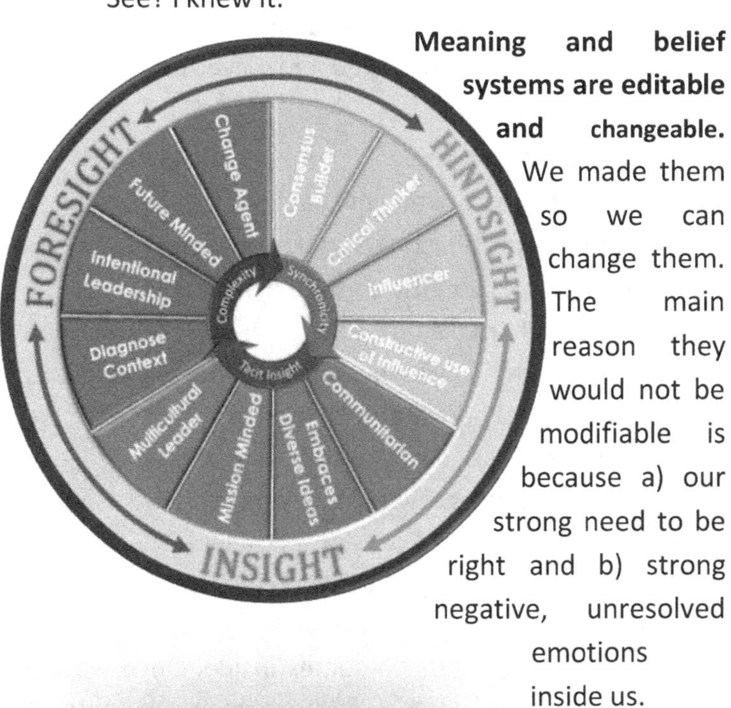

Meaning and belief systems are editable and changeable. We made them so we can change them. The main reason they would not be modifiable is because a) our strong need to be right and b) strong negative, unresolved emotions inside us.

We often make these decisions and then set out to prove to ourselves and the world that we are 'right' about whatever. Especially when working with big, negative, generalized belief systems, like "I am bad.", "the world is dangerous." and "I don't fit in", it's good to be 'wrong'.

What Makes Us Emotional?
Emotions occur in response to different kinds of stimulus (actual, imagined, or re-lived) such as:

- A physical event.
- A social interaction.
- Remembering or imagining an event.
- Talking about, thinking about, or physically reenacting a past emotional experience.

What actually makes us emotional varies by person based on our shared evolution, cultural influences and unique personal experiences. Although we cannot choose every emotion we feel, we can choose the ways in which we consciously respond, rather than react to outside events.

The Event -> Meaning -> Feeling -> Behavior Cycle (EMFB)

With EMFB, the outside comes inside. Once we are aware of this cycle, we can own it, evaluate it, process it and when   necessary, modify it and release it.

The EMFB Cycle

1. **Event:** Events happen, things happen, and keep happening throughout our life. These events mostly occur outside of us, but an illness, injury, severe physical pain, surgery, etc., the event may actually occur inside our body as well. And we must somehow try to make some sense of this.

2. **Meaning:** We bring the event inside of us by putting a meaning on what happened. Meanings are usually generalized, so statements often start with "I am..", "Life is.." and "The world is..". Words and events (only definitions) have no meanings, until we give them one.

3. **Feeling:** What we make sense of the event, which invokes feelings in us.

4. **Behavior:** Thoughts + Feelings = Actions, right?

If we have low self-esteem, our actions might be to:

a. Withdraw from others, so we won't continue to get hurt.

b. Self-medicate, since we didn't know how this process works or how to deal with the way we feel.

c. Shut-down our heart and feelings, which can cause a   host of other emotional and physical problems.

Our most significant 'life-events' generally happen

when we were very young; 3-6 years old. The details of the event are (mostly) irrelevant. It's the effect, the decision, the generalized belief systems that governed what we decided at that time. They remain with us, consciously or unconsciously affecting our thoughts, feelings, day-to-day actions & life experience going forward. To unravel this cycle, we work the steps backwards. The behaviors are almost irrelevant because they are only symptoms of the problem. Our reactions and negative thoughts will change when thoughts and feelings change.

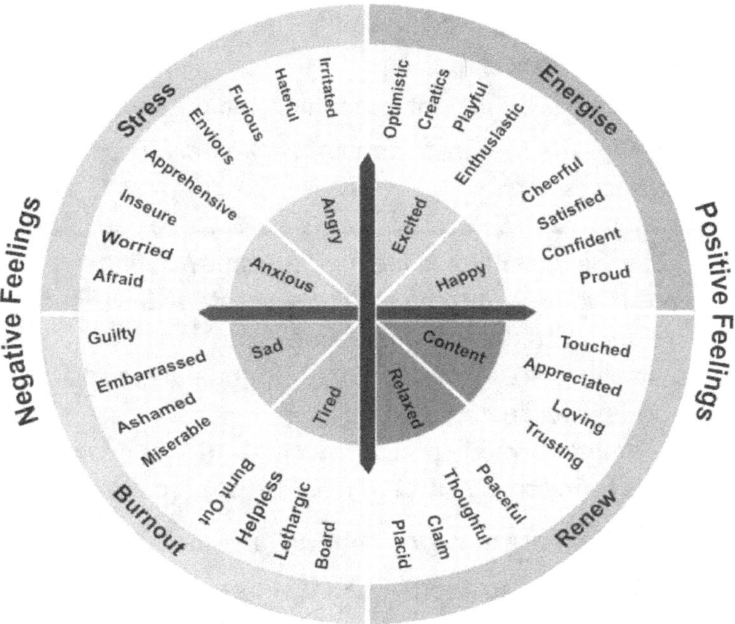

FEELINGS AND EMOTIONS

Let us start with feelings. We have unexpressed, unresolved sadness, fear and anger in our body and had to work through these, one at a time. Unresolved feelings are like glue that keeps the meanings in place. Once the feelings are fully expressed, meanings have less impact and can be made more specific and less personalized. After transforming our negative emotions to more positive ones we are able to effectively change the meanings.

- **Everything we do is for a positive need/intention for ourselves.** It may be an unwise way of achieving a goal, but it usually works.
- lead with feelings
- live with feelings
- end with feelings
- Feelings bring depth, meaning and passion to life.
- *They are the key to happiness, mental health and success in life.*

Can we feel multiple feelings at a time? Definitely.

- **Is it important to be able to separate** feelings and deal with them one at a time? Yes!
- **Feelings are all natural, organic and pure**, and are plentiful and never-ending.
- **Feelings provide critical information that our mind is trying to give us.** We need to listen to them.

- **Feelings are energy in motion**, or e-motion.

- **There are no good or bad feelings.** Although some certainly feel better than others, they can all be helpful and informative, and lend a richness and depth to life like nothing else can.

Anatomy of Emotions

- The speed of their emotional **onset** (how quickly they become emotional)
- The **frequency** of their emotions (how often they occur),
- The **intensity** of emotional response (how strong they are),
- The **duration** of the emotional response (how long they lasts),
- The **decline** of their emotional state (how long it takes to recover and go back to a baseline state).

Three Main Functions of Emotions

1. **Adaptive function** – It is important function of emotions to prepare the body for action. In this sense, each emotion, regardless of any positive or negative connotations, is useful. They help us effectively take action when needed.

2. **Social function** - Emotions communicate our emotional state of mind and express what is going on inside, while facilitating social interaction. Emotions help us predict our behavior and that of others. Due to this, emotions become useful and necessary in interpersonal relationships.

3. **Motivational function** - Emotions have a motivational function. The relationship between motivation and emotions is bidirectional with constant

feedback between emotions & motivation.

Emotional Synonyms

- Emotion, without content, or resolution = **DRAMA**
- Emotion, in order to release, and heal = **VENTING**
- Emotion, for the purpose of hurting others, getting them to 'like' you or for emotional blackmail = **MANIPULATION**
- Emotion, for the purpose of closeness, openness and intimacy = **SHARING**
- Emotion, for the purpose of making things happen and changing the world = **PASSION**
- Emotion, for the purpose of feeling fully and living fully of one's self = **EXPRESSION**
- Emotion, for the purpose of changing people, and getting them to do things your way = **CONTROL**
- Emotion, for the purpose of building boundaries, expressing values, and keeping yourself and family safe = **PERSONAL POWER**
- Emotion, for the purpose of loving, giving, understanding and healing = **COMPASSION**.

Characteristics of Emotions

- Every emotion is followed by physiological change such as rapid heartbeat, change in the pulse rate, change in blood pressure, or change in facial expression, voice and body movements.

- Emotions are subjective and purely individual. The same situation may evoke different emotions in different individuals.
- Emotion is a tri-polar response having affective, reflective & cognitive aspects.
- Emotions are wide ranging and are not restricted to a particular age group like children or adolescents.
- Emotions rise abruptly and go away quickly, however the emotional state left behind can last for some time.
- Emotions have swings. One emotion may give rise to another emotion and they may get merged.
- Emotions mostly arise when the mind faces a difficult situation or when a basic need is challenged or not satisfied. In fact, a situation real or imaginary is always connected with an emotion.
- Children's emotions are not as natural and long-standing as those of adults. Their emotions are characterized by sudden and intense outburst, are transitory, more frequent and more readily expressed or forgotten.

Negative Emotions - Acknowledge negative emotions, listen to them, learn from them, but also know that you don't have to accept them. **Emotional pain is not terminal.** We need to get 'comfortable' with our negative feelings, identify them, accept them and express them without distress and suffering.

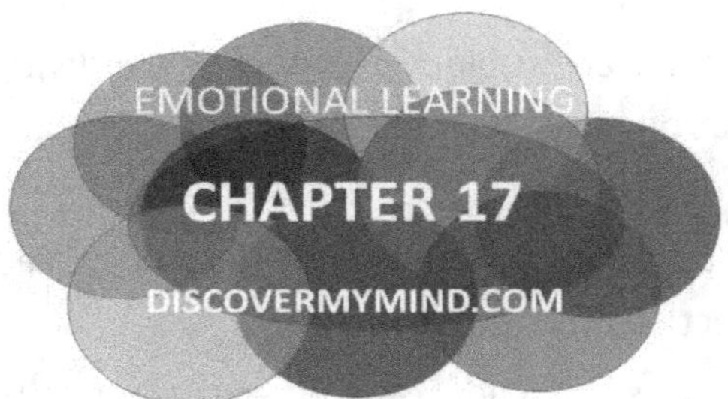

Emotional Responsibility (ER) and Emotional Ownership

Here is the reality: We create our thoughts, we generate our feelings and we choose our actions; every single one of them, every single day for the rest of our days.

The good news is that no one can *make* us feel anything emotionally without our permission. They can make us feel things physically, like a punch, a rebuke, or a handshake but they have no emotion attached.

No one 'makes' you angry, ever. You make yourself angry or more specifically, your angry thoughts make you feel angry. This realization gives you the power to make yourself 'un-angry' anytime you want to. We can control our inner world much more powerfully than you probably ever thought possible. Taking full ownership of our thoughts, feelings and actions can be painful at times, and it can be tempting to blame others for 'making' you feel a certain way hurting your feelings. However, with practice, you will find that owning your thoughts, feelings, and actions gives personal power, freedom, self-esteem, self-confidence like nothing else can.

We never do anything we don't want to do, and always have choices to choose from. You may not 'want' to do something, like get out of bed, go to school or do your chores, but you chose it, therefore you really did 'want' to do it. You can manage your thoughts and feelings. You can adjust and improve, enhance and empower. You can make great relationships or you can avoid people. You can empower yourself by using the following truths:

- I am capable
- I understand and accept cause and effect
- I know I make a difference
- I can handle delayed gratification
- I have an internal locus of control

Accepting Emotional Responsibility (ER) - Acceptance is one of the secrets to EQ. If we can train ourselves on how to accept ER quickly, completely, and powerfully, we will have made significant strides toward our inner peace. We have to accept that we have 100% complete ownership of every one of our thoughts and feelings from now on. We are in charge of them. We create them inside of us. People, places, and events can make us feel things physically but they cannot make us feel anything emotionally without our permission. We can manage our feelings, even the deepest darkest ones, adjust, improve, enhance and empower, feel and then release them. We can make great relationships or we can disassociate with people.

Accept Yourself - Self-acceptance is one of the best feelings there is. Accept you as you are, exactly as you are. Accept that you have both positive and negative emotions, and both are OK. You can fight, deny or ignore your thoughts and feelings or simply accept them as they are. Again, acceptance does not mean approval. You can accept how you are, and still want more. Acceptance means you accept yourself where you are right now.

Accept Your Thoughts, Feelings and Emotions - Accepting your feelings means accepting yourself. Suffering does not come from big emotions. Suffering comes from the resistance to emotions. Give in, allow, encourage, experience, learn from, listen to, then release, replace and rejoice. Change your judgments about your feelings from bad or neutral to good, to wow!

Accept that feelings can be uncomfortable - Learn to be comfortable being uncomfortable, as this allows you freedom. Strong feelings can be uncomfortable and even unpleasant. Make that OK inside you so you don't inhibit your growth. Others' strong feelings can also be uncomfortable. Accept them, and remain calm if they are strong feelings.

Accept without Judgment - Judgment is a step in the process of life that can be skipped completely. We need to make sense of our world and learn from our experiences. But you must know that judging people separates you from them.

Accept the Timing - Acceptance does not mean it will stay that way forever, only that it is how it is at the moment. Nothing lasts forever, including you. Timing is often not up to you. Things happen when they happen. People do what they do, when they do it.

Accept Others – Other's thoughts and feelings matter as much to them as yours matter to you, like tolerance, empathy, compassion, understanding their reality, their filters. Employ all EQ skills and concepts. Accepting others helps them accept us better.

Action or no Action – We let go when we believe we don't have control over our actions and inaction of ours. We are always 'At Choice'. If we can use all the information our mind is offering us, we can make the very best decisions for ourselves, our lives, and those we love. Once we are aware and accept what is, we can then make good, conscious, balanced, intentional, mind and heart-centered, logic and love-based, emotionally-wise decisions.

Transform Negative Emotions into Positive Ones - Validation and identification of your emotions can calm your emotional response so you can combine your thinking and feeling more effectively. When feelings go up, logic often goes down. Identifying your feelings can help your logic go back up, so your feelings are safe to come down.

Explore & Transform - Look for root causes, underlying thoughts, pain points and unconscious belief systems. Determine your options and review your choices. Decide, act or don't act, consciously. But be intentional and create the best possible outcomes.

2 Steps to Good Mental Health
1. *KNOW what you feel when you feel it* - Allow yourself to k*now*. Read, write, explore, get help, talk to others who do know -- find out what you are feeling, so you can face and deal with it. You cannot make decisions on things you are not aware of.
2. *ACCEPT what you feel when you feel it* - Learn to accept what our body feels as real, natural, honest, and good!

Again, acceptance does not mean approval.

Change your judgments on your feelings from bad to good, in your mind. Decide that feelings are the key to healing and that they must be acknowledged and expressed, not avoided and stuffed, even though they can be uncomfortable or unpleasant.

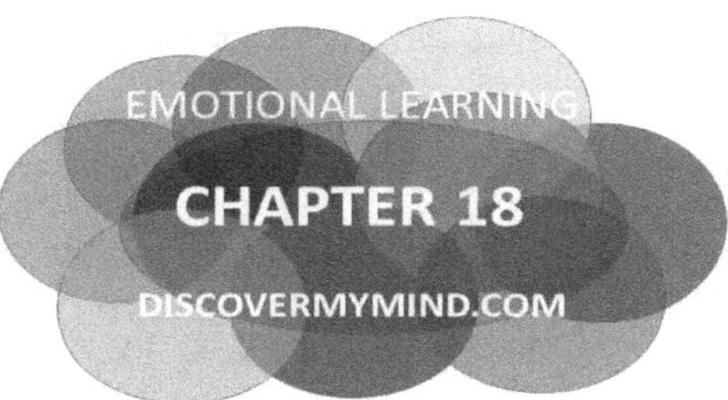

Components of Effective Decision-Making

Getting Better Results - With better actions come better results.

- Increased collaboration and connections

- Providing psychological safety

- Reduced miscommunications, hurt feelings and distancing

- Improved emphasis on relationships and inclusion

- Enhanced problem-solving

- Increased empathy and compassion

- Build more cohesive families and personal support networks

- Enhanced awareness, understanding and agility

- Ensuring thorough and compassionate responses

- Adaptability and flexibility to changing environments

5 Action Strategies for Improving our EQ

- Pay more attention to your emotions on a daily basis

- Improve your non-verbal communication and become sensitive to those of others

- Practice empathy

- Exercise self-regulation.

- Sharpen your social skills

When we have a problem or issue, we can make the problem seem much worse by doing one or more of the following:

- **Permanence:** Thinking a bad situation will last forever. Those who think setbacks are only temporary have improved ability to accept and adapt for the future.

- **Pervasiveness:** Thinking a bad situation applies across all areas of your life, instead of happening in one area only. People who think bad situations are pervasive feel that multiple areas of their life are impacted. This can make it hard to carry on.

- **Personalization:** Believing that the problem is you, instead of considering other things or people that could have caused it. Defining how outside factors may have caused a bad situation allows us to reduce the blame and criticism we put on ourselves.

- A pessimist and optimist view the same situation differently. A pessimist sees things as permanent, pervasive and personal.

- An optimist will see things as temporary, isolated and with effort; the situation can be improved (powerful, not powerless).

- A pessimist can take an opportunity and make it into a difficulty. An optimist can take a difficulty and make it into an opportunity.

- Manage the negatives but accentuate the positives. Be specific; don't make it Pervasive your whole life.

- The situation is probably not permanent.

Be Impeccable with your Word - Speak with integrity. Say only what you mean. Use the power of your word to the direction of truth and love. Above all, keep your word.

Don't Take Anything Personally - Nothing others do is because of you. What others say and do is a projection of their own reality, their own dream. When you are immune to the opinions and actions of others, you won't be the victim of needless suffering.

Don't Make Assumptions - Find the courage to ask questions and to express what you really want. Communicate with others as clearly as you can to avoid misunderstandings and drama. With just this one agreement, you can completely transform your life.

Always Do Your Best - Your best is going to change from moment to moment. Under any circumstance, simply do your best and you will avoid self- judgment, disappointment and regret.

Learn To Listen - Don't believe yourself or anybody else without good reason. Use the power of doubt to question what you hear: Is it really the truth? Listen to the intent behind the words, and you will understand the real message.

Empathy - Empathy isn't just about feeling sorry for someone. That is sympathy.
* True empathy is about really understanding and connecting with others.
* Empathy allows us to connect at a deeper level by opening up our heart.
* We can see the world the way others do and without judgment.

* There are three types of Empathy.
1. Cognitive Empathy - think and understand what they think.
2. Emotional Empathy - feel what they feel, mirror neurons.
3. Empathic Concern - feel compelled to help
* Practice feeling empathy for yourself and others

0 Practice tuning in to yourself, and having compassion and understanding for your inner child.

0 Practice tuning in to the feelings of others.

0 Assume people are doing the best they can and are struggling with unseen issues we are unaware of.

0 Learn and practice the essential elements of dialogue, and initiate conversations during times of stress.

0 Practice listening without interrupting.

0 Get to know people: family, friends, classmates, team mates on a personal level

0 Listen to, understand and connect, not just to respond. Understanding the question first, is half the answer.

The 5 C's of Trust – Care - People will trust and support you if they know you truly care about them. Caring can show up in how you connect with others. Caring leaders give credit to their employees and challenge them to reach new levels. When we care, we lead with the heart and the head.

What does care look and sound like to you?

Commitment - Showing up punctually is an essential part of the commitment. It means bringing energy and initiative to the job. It means staying on the course and doing what you say you will do, long after the time when you first said it. Keep your commitments no matter how small or large. If you can't keep a commitment, you have to communicate this and ask to be released from it.

Consistency: Consistent leaders evaluate themselves and make sure their words and actions are congruent. Decide what your values are and use them to make decisions. It will help to guide you and keep you consistent.

Competence: People will question your competence if they don't see it in action. When people can see that you know what you are doing, they extend trust. Your competence is developed through experience and requires a lot of hard work.

Communication: Communication is the exchange of information. You are not communicating until the other person understands what you are saying. Trust gives you the ability to communicate in a caring, committed, consistent and competent way.

Positive Conscious - We have plenty of unconscious negatives. To take control of happiness, add conscious positives to your life.

- Love, empathy & compassion

- Gratitude, thankfulness & appreciation

- Calm, peace and serenity

- Giving, receiving and being kind

- Joy, humor and laughter

- Feeling happy for no reason

- Take conscious and intentional actions, and add positive feelings on purpose like relaxing, smiling, playing, laughing etc.

Listening carefully to your self-talk, as the words and thoughts you choose, will point to your underlying belief systems.
- Be aware of all-or-nothing thoughts, negative labels you call yourself and mind-reading.
- Seek, find, examine, evaluate, specify, modify and enhance your internal belief systems.
- Be especially cognizant of your generalized beliefs.
- Also, listen to yourself and notice how your beliefs and self- talk emerge while communicating with others.

Utilize an assertive style of communicating - Emotionally intelligent people know how to communicate their opinions and needs in a direct way, respecting the needs of others.

9 Habits of Highly Emotionally Intelligent People

1. They are relentlessly positive.
2. They have a robust emotional vocabulary.
3. They are assertive.
4. They are curious about things.
5. They forgive but they don't forget.
6. They don't let anyone limit their joy.
7. They make things fun.
8. They are difficult to offend.
9. They quash negative self-talk.

Responding instead of reacting to conflict - The emotionally intelligent person knows how to stay calm during stressful situations, and they don't make impulsive decisions that can lead to even bigger problems. They understand that in times of conflict, the goal is resolution, and that that is where the focus remains.

Utilize active listening skills - In conversations, emotionally intelligent people listen for clarity and make sure they understand what is being said before responding. They also pay attention to nonverbal details, which allows the listener to respond properly and shows respect for the speaker.

Stay motivated - Emotionally intelligent people are self-motivated, set goals, resilient in the face of challenges. This attitude motivates others.

Practice ways to maintain a positive attitude - Emotionally intelligent people have an awareness of the moods of those around them and govern their attitude accordingly.

Practice self-awareness - Emotionally intelligent people are intuitive and aware of their own emotions, and how they can affect those around them. They also observe the interaction to enhance their communication skills.

Take critique well - Instead of getting offended or defensive, high EQ people take a few moments to understand where the critique is coming from, how it is affecting others or their own performance, and how to constructively resolve the issues.

Empathize with others - Emotionally intelligent people understand that empathy is a trait that shows emotional strength, not weakness, and helps them to relate to others at a basic human level.

Utilize leadership skills - Emotionally intelligent people have high standards for themselves and set an example for others to follow. They take initiative and have great decision making and problem-solving skills.

Be approachable and sociable - Emotionally intelligent people come off as friendly, kind, caring, safe and approachable.

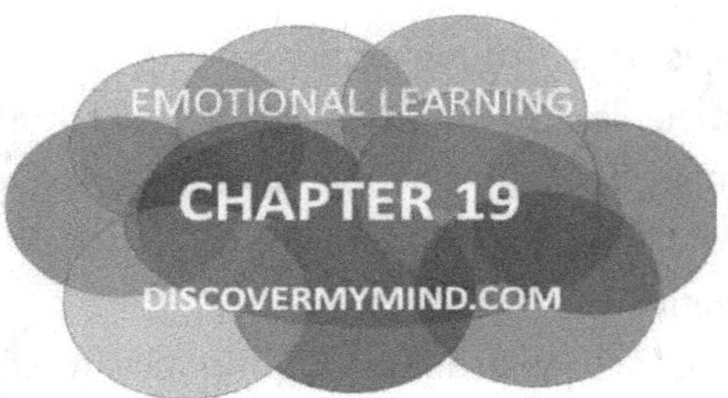

Conflict Management

When conflict inevitably happens, respectful communication is the key. You may not always agree with everyone, but polite words and an open mind can help you resolve — or come to terms with - differences more effectively.

To avoid blaming, complaining and withdrawal, use "I" statements as much as possible. Instead of saying, "You did X," or "You always Y," try something like, "I have a hard time when X" or "I feel Y."

NVC - Nonviolent Communications is a worldwide organization developing and teaching ways to communicate that are peaceful, effective, and above all, non- violent.

The NVC teachings and organization helps people connect with each other and themselves in a way that allows natural compassion to flourish. It guides us to reframe the way we express ourselves and listen to others by focusing our consciousness on four areas: what we are observing, feeling, and needing, and what we are requesting to enrich our lives.

NVC fosters deep listening, respect and empathy,

and engenders a mutual desire to give from the heart. Some people use NVC to respond compassionately to themselves, some to create greater depth in their personal relationships, and still others to build effective relationships at work or in the political arena.

7 Rules for Dealing with Interpersonal Conflict
1. Acknowledge the conflict
2. Open up the lines of communication
3. Focus on the problem, not the other person
4. Stick to the facts
5. Meet face to face (if possible)
6. Choose your battles
7. Make a decision and act on it

Being Present Now - Not living in fear of the future, but being here, now, and in the present. Here are some tips on 'Being present' from Positive Psychology:

- Notice your judgments about yourself and about others.

- Practice noticing and naming your experiences.

- Focus on and picture what you want, not what you don't want.

- Recognize that other people are simply a mirror of yourself.

- Practice awareness by noticing the stories you

create and your interpretation of them.

- Practice unbundling your feelings, making them more specific so you can manage them one-at-a time.

- Notice the degree with which your emotions, thoughts and wants are positive or negative.

Building Trust

Trust is a vital component to EQ. Trust is a firm belief in the reliability, truth, ability and strength of someone or something.

Notice your level of trust in your important relationships. Identify people who helped shape your viewpoint and/or trust, both positively and negatively. Pay attention to the degree that you trust yourself (or don't) in important relationships. Practice inviting feedback from others. Ask. Act as if you really count in a conversation (*hint: you do!*). Notice when you tend to criticize yourself without reason. Get to know the people who are important to you. Practice asking for help and assistance and/or delegating to others. Assume but verify that other people's intentions are positive and in your best interests.

The three requirements for a successful relationship: To be successful, it is helpful if both parties have:
1. A willingness to create an emotionally 'safe' environment where they share their feelings honestly and accept the other's feelings without

judgment.

2. A win-win, problem-solving attitude in which neither one loses. Some say relationships are 50/50, but they work better if both are 100% responsible for the relationship.

3. Have similar values.

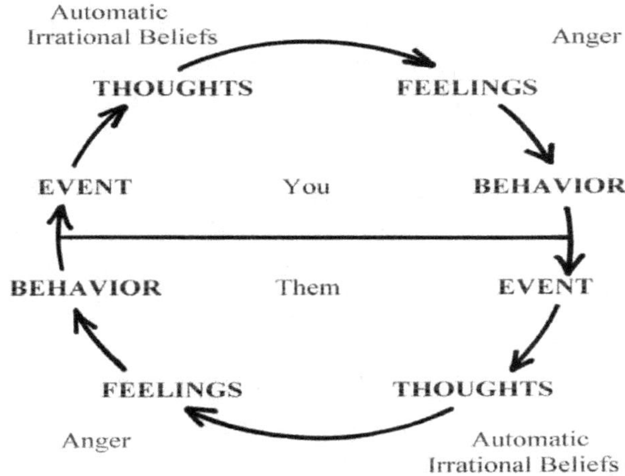

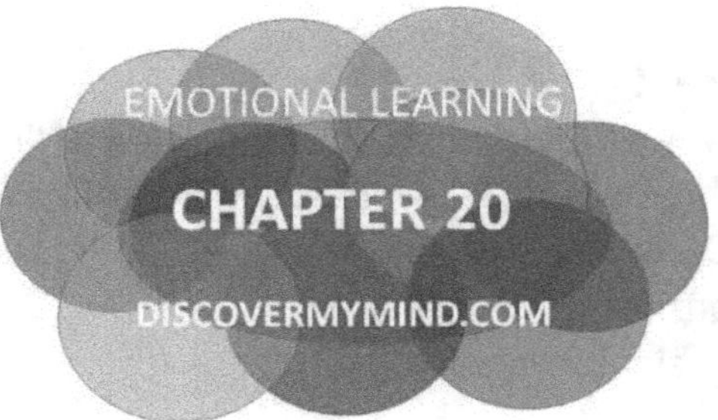

Communications, Listening and Learning
Verbal Communications

If you get your feelings hurt by something someone said or did, before taking action ask if they 'meant' to hurt your feelings or not? Most of the time, they were unaware and did not mean to hurt you and will often apologize. However if they did mean to hurt you, a wholly different conversation or action is recommended.

EQ is sometimes about being brave enough to ask tough questions that need to be asked. When trying to help someone feel better, listen for and ask about their feelings specifically. The details, their opinions, their judgments, even their actions are mostly irrelevant. The key is to help them realize, name, separate, accept, understand and take responsibility for their feelings and emotions. The biggest thing is to ask, "what thought(s) did you have, that created that/those feelings?" From there, you can often help them think about a subject in a different way that is less generalized, less personalized, specific, clear, understanding with empathy and compassion. You are not your emotions. Instead of "I *am* angry", try saying, "I *feel* angry". This gives you more credit, more power and control.

If you want to talk for 'real', not just about the weather, talk and ask about, 'feelings'. Take full and complete responsibility for them, and where appropriate, ask about theirs.

- Accentuate the positives in your relationship, especially your positive feelings toward the person, or your time together

- Establish rapport!

- Ask "what are you feeling?", rather than "How are you?"

- Distinguish between the behavior and the person as a whole. We can despise a behavior, and still love the person. Be hard on the behavior, go soft on the person.

- People are going to do what they do, not what you think they should or not do.

Non-Verbal Communications - Facial expressions, body language, tone of voice, eye contact, physical proximity, wording, energy, touch/avoidance are all relevant non-verbal communications. Much of our intention, energy and attitude can come across non-verbally. Some say we portray much more non-verbally as we do verbally.

Listening Skills - Often, the **#1 best gift** you can give someone is an open listening, accepting ear, and your time.

▌ SOUL Technique: **S: S**top - stop what you are doing, stop talking - **O: O**pen - **U: U**p your heart - **L: L**isten

▌ SOLER Technique: **S: S**it - **O: O**pen posture - **L: L**ean slightly forward - **E:** maintain **E**ye contact, be sensitive; people are uncomfortable with extended eye-contact. – **R: R**elax & pay attention

Tips on Listening:

- Encourage venting (emotional responsibility), while discouraging complaining.
- Celebrate emotionally responsible attitudes and behavior.
- Show you're listening, even with small sounds,

noises or "hmmm." or "yes" or "I see."
- Ask, "What were your biggest feelings when that happened?" "What do you feel about it now?"
- Ask, "What do you see as your options?" and help them explore additional options and/or decide on the best option(s) to pursue.
- Ask, "How bad is it?" Try rating your pain on a scale of 1-10.
- Paraphrase - Restate what you heard them say and ask if you heard them correctly. If not, ask that they try saying it again.
- Ask yourself, why are they telling me this? What are they trying to get across to me?
- Ask how you can be helpful and what outcome they would like.
- Don't be condescending or tell them not to worry, and be careful of "look at the bright side..."
- Don't give unsolicited advice *(NOTE: this is harder than it sounds)*
- Don't compare yourself to others, "you think that's bad, others have it worse than you." *(Note: yes, they think it's that's bad)*
- Don't interrupt or talk over them.
- Don't tell them to think about something else. (they won't)

The most basic of all human needs is the need to understand and be understood. The best way to understand people is to listen to them. –
Ralph G. Nichols

The Anatomy of Conflict:
If there is no communication then there is no respect.
If there is no respect then there is no caring.
If there is no caring then there is no understanding. If there is no understanding then there is no compassion.
If there is no compassion then there is no empathy. If there is no empathy then there is no forgiveness. If there is no forgiveness then there is no kindness. If there is no kindness then there is no honesty.
If there is no honesty then there is no love.
If there is no love, we have nothing

"Educating the mind without educating the heart is no education at all". – Aristotle

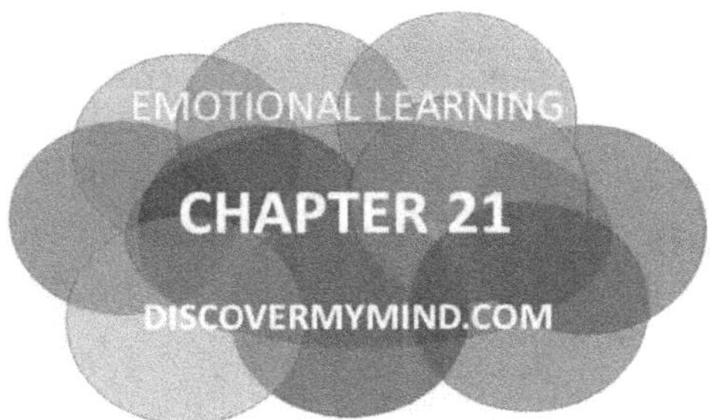

Impact of EI on the Human Resource Function

Emotional intelligence is the "something" in each of us that is a bit intangible. It affects how we manage behavior, navigate social complexities, and make personal decisions that achieve desired results. Emotional intelligence is made up of core skills that pair up under two primary competencies: personal competence and social competence.

Personal competence is made up of your self-awareness and self-management skills, which focus more on you individually than on your interactions with other people. Personal competence is your ability to stay aware of your emotions and manage your behavior and tendencies.

- *Self-Awareness* is your ability to accurately perceive your emotions and stay aware of them as they happen.
- *Self-Management* - ability to use awareness of emotions to stay flexible and positively direct behavior.
- *Social competence* is made up of your social

awareness and relationship management skills; social competence is your ability to understand other people's moods, behavior, and motives in order to improve the quality of your relationships.

- *Social Awareness* is your ability to accurately pick up on emotions in other people and understand what is really going on.
- *Relationship Management* is your ability to use awareness of your emotions and the others' emotions to manage interactions successfully.

Emotional Intelligence, IQ, and Personality Are Different - Emotional intelligence taps into a fundamental element of human behavior that is distinct from your intellect. There is no known connection between IQ and emotional intelligence; you simply can't predict emotional intelligence based on how smart someone is. Intelligence is your ability to learn, and it's the same at age 5 as it is at age 50.

Emotional intelligence, on the other hand, is a flexible set of skills that can be acquired and improved with practice. Although some people are naturally more emotionally intelligent than others, you can develop this even if you aren't born with it.

Personality is the final piece of the puzzle. It's the stable "style" that defines each of us. Personality is the result of hard-wired preferences, such as the inclination toward introversion or extroversion. However, like IQ, personality can't be used to predict emotional intelligence. Also, personality is stable over a lifetime and doesn't change.

Emotional Intelligence Is Performance-Linked - Emotional intelligence is the foundation for a host of critical skills—it impacts almost everything we say and do each day. Emotional intelligence is the single biggest predictor of performance in the workplace, and the strongest driver of leadership and personal excellence. The link between emotional intelligence and earnings is so direct that every point increase in emotional intelligence adds a large sum to an annual salary. These findings hold true for people in all industries, at all levels, in every region of the world.

We haven't yet been able to find a job in which performance and pay aren't tied closely to emotional intelligence. *Emotional intelligence is the foundation for critical skills.*

Emotional Intelligence Can Be Developed - The communication between your emotional and rational "brains" is the physical source of emotional intelligence. The pathway for emotional intelligence starts in the brain, at the spinal cord. Your primary senses enter here and must travel to the front of your brain before you can think rationally about your experience. However, first, they travel through the limbic system, the place where emotions are generated. So, we have an emotional reaction to events before our rational mind can engage. Emotional intelligence requires effective communication between the rational and emotional centers of the brain.

Emotional intelligence is a balance between the rational and the *emotional brain.*

The reason IQ by itself is not a very good predictor of job performance is because education and hiring practices weed out those who can't master what they need to know on the job. Most physicians who pass their boards and go on to practice medicine are similarly qualified. The same is true of lawyers, sales professionals, administrative assistants, and most professions you can name.

What makes one person shine over another and what *does* predict job performance is the combination of a person's ability to learn (IQ), who that person is (personality), and how they handle themselves and others on the job (EQ).

Emotional Intelligence is the third major contributor to a person's success. It is made up of personal and social competence skills: self-awareness, self-management, social awareness and relationship management.

What is it about EQ skills that impact a person's job performance? Whether we are aware of them or not, emotions surface in everything we think, do, and say each day. Awareness of our own emotions and tendencies opens doors for us to manage ourselves more effectively (Self-Management) by making better decisions, and responding to challenges productively and proactively. Awareness of the emotions in other people (Social Awareness), including unspoken cues, enables us to influence others and build and deepen relationships more effectively (Relationship Management). Employees who increase their EQ skills increase their ability to communicate effectively, make good decisions, handle conflict, be a team player, respond to change well, handle stress better and provide top-notch customer service.

Emotional intelligence is a highly flexible skill. With practice, people who measure low in EQ can work to improve a specific EQ skill within 6 months to a year. During the last two decades, research shows that people who develop their emotional intelligence tend to be successful on the job because the two go hand in hand. These findings hold true for people in a variety of professions across industries, at all levels, all over the world.

Organizations who were early adopters, working to increase the EQ of their workforce, reaped tremendous benefits that garnered significant media attention in the 1990s, including The Harvard Business Review's most popular piece of all time (What Makes a Leader?). EQ skills can be improved, yet they are not typically taught in college or post-graduate degree programs. Companies who teach these skills to their workforce achieve tremendous gains. Now, major corporations, universities and government agencies are making emotional intelligence an integral part of their employee training, talent development and leadership development initiatives.

'Plasticity' is the term neurologists use to describe the brain's ability to change. Your brain grows new connections as you learn new skills. The change is gradual, as your brain cells develop new connections to speed the efficiency of new skills acquired.

Using strategies to increase your emotional intelligence allows the billions of microscopic neurons lining the road between the rational and emotional centers of your brain to branch off small "arms" (much like a tree) to reach out to the other cells. A single cell can grow 15,000 connections with its neighbors.

This chain reaction of growth ensures ongoing development of our neural pathways.

CONCLUSION

Paradigm changes are happening across the world in terms of finding learning outcomes in our education system other than in the outdated instruction set in practice today. It is becoming clear that a new quantum theory in the area of behavioral science is unfolding, provoking a radical new examination of the impact of EI on emotional health. Eminent speakers in academia and social media are presenting fascinating insight as to what might be almost a catharsis to our present way of thinking.

There are three main takeaways from this book.

Firstly, we must mount an education and awareness campaign on the value and benefits of personal profiling and assessment as a means of ensuring emotional health. Secondly, we must ensure that all schools and colleges have at least one trained and certified Counselor on EI to provide the best Counseling. And finally, psychotherapists in our country must embrace and implement emotional learning as an integral part of their practice, much more so than at present.

While the focus of the book is on the education space, all tenets and content apply to mental health professionals, trainers, coaches and Counselors in all areas of behavior management.

Many people confuse emotional intelligence and intelligence quotient. When you can learn how to command your emotions, you will be able to exercise greater control over your life and ultimately unlock opportunities that would have otherwise remained hidden. High emotional intelligence is something that everyone should be working hard to obtain. This means that you shouldn't be discouraged and sidetracked, but rather, you need to continue to press on and aggressively pursue your emotional goals.

Emotional intelligence teaches and trains you how to better relate with the people around you. With the pace at which the world is quickly becoming a global village, it is more important now that you learn how to listen and interpret the information that you are gathering from those around you. By doing this, you can learn how to structure your response and communicate better with those around you. When you have higher emotional intelligence, you will ultimately find success in both your personal and professional life.

Appendices

Appendix 1

Emotional Intelligence – Self Assessment

This questionnaire is a useful starting tool for reviewing current level of Emotional Intelligence. Please note that the results don't give you a comprehensive picture of your Emotional Intelligence. Tick each of the statements that accurately describe how you behave at work. Do make sure that your appraisal is honest.

1. I am aware when I start to get angry or defensive.
2. When I am dealing with an angry person, I keep relaxed and focused on my goals.
3. I remain cheerful and enjoy working on new ideas.
4. I follow through on assignments, support   others and build trust.
5. Despite setbacks and problems, I   work in a calm manner.
6. I use positive thinking, even when I am in a conflict or a difficult situation.
7. I can feel and see things from different viewpoints.
8. I clearly understand the strengths and   weaknesses of my behavior.
9. I practice stress management to be calm and healthy.
10. When I communicate with others, I help them feel good.
11. Before I make a decision or take an action, I listen

to others' ideas.

12. I can sense how a work colleague is feeling without saying much to him/her.
13. To resolve conflicts, I encourage honest and respectful discussion.
14. I help people who hold different opinions to reach agreement.
15. I inspire others to achieve challenging goals.
16. When I am making changes, I consider the other's feelings.
17. I am aware of when I start to think negatively
18. I have a good sense of humor
19. I am confident that I can achieve a task once I apply myself to it.
20. I can get back on track quickly after I   become emotionally upset.

This questionnaire doesn't give you a score, but it gives you a snapshot at your current level of EI and helps you focus on your state of emotions when dealing with certain situations.

<u>Appendix 2</u>

MULTIPLE INTELLIGENCES CHECKLIST

It is hoped that this checklist will be fun to do and will help you discover your many gifts. This is not a test – it's just for your own information – but it is based on wonderful studies done by many wise people about how we learn and why it is really great to know our own preferences; each one of us is unique and our preferences help us understand our special ways of learning and knowing.

Check any items that seem to apply to you. You may check as   many as you like. Please have a good time and enjoy yourself!

1. I enjoy reading books.
2. I have always liked math and science classes best and I do well in them.
3. I enjoy drawing, painting and doodling.
4. I love being outdoors and enjoy spending my free time outside.
5. I have a pleasant singing voice and I like to sing.
6. I'm the kind of person others come to for advice.
7. I have some important goals for my life that I think about often.
8. I love animals and I spend a lot of time with them.
9. I like English, social studies and history better than math and science.
10. I try to look for patterns and regularities in things,

such as every third stair on the staircase has a notch in it.

11. I like to figure out how to take apart and put back together things like toys and puzzles.
12. I am an active person and if I can't move around I get bored.
13. I frequently listen to music because I enjoy it so much.
14. I like going to parties and social events.
15. I think I am a very independent person.
16. I enjoy watching nature shows on television.
17. I am good at using words to get others to change their mind.
18. I enjoy playing around with a chemistry set and am interested in new discoveries in science.
19. When I watch a movie or video, I am more interested in what I see than what I hear.
20. I think I am well coordinated.
21. I can play a musical instrument.
22. I don't like to argue with people.
23. Sometimes I talk to myself.
24. It's fun to watch birds or other animals, to watch their habits, and to learn more about them.
25. I'm good at Scrabble and other word games.
26. I believe that almost everything has a logical explanation.
27. When I close my eyes, sometimes I can see clear images in my head that seem real.
28. I have good skills in one or more sports and learn new sports quickly.

29. I can easily keep time to a piece of music.
30. I enjoy getting other people to work together.
31. I like to spend time alone thinking about things that are important to me.
32. I'm very good at telling the difference between different kinds of birds, dogs, trees and stuff like that.
33. I like to learn new words and know their meanings.
34. I like to play games and solve brainteasers that require tactics and strategy.
35. I am good at reading maps and finding my way around unfamiliar places.
36. I don't like organized team sports as much as individual sports activities, such as tennis, swimming, skiing, golf or ballet.
37. I know the tunes and titles of many songs and musical pieces.
38. I consider myself a leader (and others call me that).
39. I would rather spend a vacation in a cabin in the woods than at a fancy resort.
40. I enjoy visiting zoos, natural history museums or other places where the world is studied.
41. It's easy for me to memorize things at school.
42. It is fun for me to work with numbers and data.
43. I like some colors better than others.
44. I don't mind getting my hands dirty from activities like painting, clay modeling, or fixing and building things.
45. Sometimes I catch myself walking along with a television jingle or song in my mind.

46. When I have a problem, I'll probably ask a friend for help.
47. I think I know what I am good at and what I'm not so good at doing.
48. I like being outside whenever possible; I feel confident and comfortable there.
49. I like to look things up in the dictionary or any encyclopedia.
50. I like to ask people questions about how things work or   why nature is the way it is.
51. I sketch or draw when I think.
52. Sometimes when I talk with people, I gesture with my hands.
53. I like to make up my own tunes and melodies.
54. I have at least three close friends.
55. I have hobbies and interests that I prefer to do on my own.
56. I like camping and hiking.
57. I like to talk to friends and family better than watching TV.
58. I have an easy time understanding new math concepts in school.
59. I enjoy reading things more when they have lots of pictures and drawings.
60. I would rather play a sport than watch it.
61. Often I keep time to music by tapping to the beat or humming the tune when I am studying or talking on the phone.
62. I am easy to get to know.
63. I want to be self-employed or maybe start my own

business.

64. I want to become a volunteer in an ecological organization (such as Greenpeace or Sierra Club) to help save nature from further destruction.
65. I like to write things like stories, poems and reports.
66. I like things better when they are organized, categorized or measured.
67. I am good at playing Pictionary, doing jigsaw puzzles, and solving mazes.
68. I like to "ham it up" in skits, plays, speeches, sports or other types of activities.
69. I can tell when notes are off-key.
70. I feel comfortable most of the time, even in the midst of a crowd.
71. I like to spend time by myself thinking about thing that I value.
72. When I was younger I used to dislodge big rocks from the ground to discover the living things underneath.
73. I'm really good at describing things in words.
74. I think I am good at working with numbers and data.
75. I am better at remembering faces than names.
76. I like working with my hands in activities such as sewing, carving, or model-building.
77. I know what I like and don't like in music.
78. I am good at making new friends.
79. I like to think about things before I take any action.
80. I have a green thumb and I am really good at

keeping   plants alive and healthy.

TALLY SHEET

Circle the numbers below that you checked on your Multiple Intelligence checklist. Then count how many circles you have in each column, and write that number at the bottom of each column.

Look at the columns where you counted the most circles. You may have one, two or three areas that stand out. It doesn't matter how many, but rather what "fits" and seems right for you. See the key below to discover your natural preferences!

LIN = Linguistic   MU = Musical
LM = Logical-Mathematical   NTER = Interpersonal
SP = Spatial   NTRA = Intrapersonal
BK = Bodily-Kinesthetic   NAT = Naturalist

You are a unique and special individual with many wonderful abilities, gifts and talents!

	1	2	3	4	5	6	7	8
	9	1	1	1	1	1	1	1
	1	1	1	2	2	2	2	2
	2	2	2	2	2	3	3	3
	3	3	3	3	3	3	3	4
	4	4	4	4	4	4	4	4
	4	5	5	5	5	5	5	5
	5	5	5	6	6	6	6	6
	6	6	6	6	6	7	7	7
	7	7	7	7	7	7	7	8
How many *circles* in each column?								
	LIN	IM	SP	BK	MU	NTER	NTRA	NAT

Contact Information

Email: eqtraining@discovermymind.com Mob: +91

9958960437

Website: www.discovermymind.com
Editorial Inspiration:

Ms. Lata Singh, Director, MEQ Academy.
Ms. Annapurna A. Swaroop, President,

Emotionalytics. Dr. Hemant Lawanghare, Dean,

Emotional Intelligence MBA program, Bombay University.

* 9 7 9 8 4 3 7 4 4 8 8 9 2 *